LOW CARB HIGH PROTEIN MEAL PREP

2000 Days of Simple, Healthy, and Delicious Recipes for Weight Loss and Muscle Building

Debbie Raistrick

Table of contents

Chapter 5: Top Muscle: Nutritious Delights to Rejuvenate You............73

Chapter 6: Recovery Day Recipes.103

Chapter 7: Various Recipes..........125

Introduction

Welcome to "Low Carb High Protein Meal Prep: 2000 Days of Simple, Healthy, and Delicious Recipes for Weight Loss and Muscle Building." This cookbook is designed to guide you through the transformative benefits of a low-carb, high-protein diet, empowering you to achieve your health and fitness goals with ease and enjoyment.

A low-carb, high-protein diet offers numerous health benefits. Reducing carbohydrate intake can stabilise blood sugar levels, decrease inflammation, and improve metabolic health. High protein intake supports muscle repair and growth, boosts metabolism, and helps you feel fuller for longer, reducing the temptation to overeat.

One of the most significant impacts of this diet is weight loss. Reducing carbs can decrease insulin levels, causing your body to burn stored fat for energy. Meanwhile, a high protein intake preserves lean muscle mass, ensuring that the weight you lose is primarily fat. This dual approach makes it easier to achieve and maintain a healthy weight.

Building muscle is another critical advantage of this diet. Protein provides the essential amino acids needed for muscle synthesis, which is particularly beneficial for those engaged in regular physical activity. Whether lifting weights, swimming, or participating in any other form of exercise, a high-protein diet will support your muscle-building efforts and enhance recovery.

Throughout this cookbook, you'll find testimonials and success stories from individuals who have embraced a low-carb, high-protein lifestyle. Their experiences highlight this dietary approach's practical and long-term benefits, offering inspiration and motivation as you embark on your journey.

Embark on this culinary adventure with us and discover how delicious, nutritious, and fulfilling a low-carb, high-protein diet can be. Let's make every meal a step toward a healthier, stronger you.

The Benefits of a Low-Carb and High-Protein Diet

Embarking on a low-carb, high-protein diet offers many benefits that can transform your health and lifestyle. This dietary approach is not just a trend; it's a sustainable way to improve overall well-being, achieve weight loss goals, and build muscle effectively.

One of the primary health benefits of a low-carb, high-protein diet is its powerful role in stabilising blood sugar levels. Minimising carbohydrate intake reduces the spikes and crashes in blood glucose, often leading to cravings and overeating. This stabilisation helps manage insulin levels, decreasing the risk of type 2 diabetes and enhancing overall metabolic health. Additionally, lower carb intake can significantly reduce inflammation in the body, a key factor in numerous chronic diseases, including heart disease and arthritis. This reduction in inflammation can provide reassurance and confidence in the diet's health benefits.

Weight loss is a significant impact of this diet. Reducing carbs forces your body to burn stored fat for energy, leading to more efficient fat loss. High protein intake plays a crucial role here as well. Protein increases satiety, making you feel fuller for extended periods and naturally reducing calorie intake. Furthermore, it boosts your metabolism, aiding in faster calorie burn. This combination of fat-burning and increased metabolism makes weight loss more achievable and sustainable.

Building muscle is another essential benefit. Protein, the hero of this diet, provides the necessary amino acids for muscle repair and growth, which is particularly beneficial for those who engage in regular physical activity. A diet rich in protein supports muscle synthesis, enhances recovery, and helps maintain lean muscle mass while losing fat. Whether you're a professional athlete or just enjoy regular exercise, a high-protein diet can significantly enhance your performance and recovery.

Throughout this journey, you will find inspiration in the testimonials and success stories of individuals who have embraced this lifestyle. Their experiences serve as a testament to the practicality and effectiveness of a low-carb, high-protein diet. These stories highlight significant weight loss and muscle gains and improvements in energy levels, mood, and overall quality of life.

Adopting a low-carb, high-protein diet is a decisive step toward a healthier, more vibrant you. It's about making informed food choices that support your body's needs while enjoying delicious, satisfying meals. Whether you're aiming to lose weight, build muscle, or improve your health, this diet offers a balanced and enjoyable approach to eating that can be sustained for the long term.

Health Benefits

A low-carb, high-protein diet provides numerous health benefits beyond weight loss and muscle building. This dietary approach can profoundly affect various bodily systems, enhancing overall health and well-being. Understanding the anatomical processes can help you appreciate why this diet is particularly beneficial.

When you consume fewer carbohydrates, your body enters a metabolic state known as ketosis. In ketosis, the liver converts fat into fatty acids and ketone bodies, which are then used as the primary energy sources instead of glucose. This shift promotes fat loss and leads to more stable blood sugar levels. Stable blood sugar levels prevent insulin resistance, a precursor to type 2 diabetes. Maintaining lower and more consistent blood glucose levels reduces the risk of developing this chronic condition.

Proteins, the building blocks of our body, play a critical role in cell repair and growth. A high protein intake supports the maintenance and repair of tissues, including muscles, skin, and organs. Proteins are composed of amino acids, which are essential for the synthesis of enzymes and hormones. These enzymes and hormones regulate various bodily functions, including metabolism, immune response, and mood stabilisation. For instance, the amino acid tryptophan is a precursor to serotonin, a neurotransmitter that contributes to feelings of well-being and happiness.

Furthermore, high-protein diets have been shown to impact heart health positively. Studies suggest that reducing carbohydrate intake and increasing protein consumption can improve lipid profiles. This means lower levels of bad cholesterol (LDL) and triglycerides and higher levels of good cholesterol (HDL). These changes reduce the risk of cardiovascular diseases, such as heart attacks and strokes. A protein-rich diet can also help lower blood pressure, protecting against heart disease.

A high-protein, low-carb diet also benefits digestive health. Protein-rich foods often contain essential nutrients and fibre, which promote healthy digestion. Fibre aids in regular bowel movements and prevents constipation while supporting the growth of beneficial gut bacteria.

A healthy gut microbiome is linked to improved immune function, reduced inflammation, and better mental health.

Despite common misconceptions, this diet positively affects kidney function. For healthy individuals, a high protein intake does not harm the kidneys. Instead, it supports their function by helping to filter blood and excrete waste products efficiently. However, those with pre-existing kidney conditions should consult their healthcare provider before significantly increasing protein intake.

Lastly, a diet low in carbs and high in protein can boost mental clarity and cognitive function. Stable blood sugar levels prevent the energy crashes that can affect concentration and mood. Proteins provide the necessary amino acids for neurotransmitter production, supporting cognitive processes and emotional balance.

The health benefits of a low-carb, high-protein diet are extensive and multifaceted. By promoting stable blood sugar levels, supporting tissue repair and hormone production, improving heart and digestive health, and enhancing mental clarity, this dietary approach offers a comprehensive strategy for improving overall health and well-being. Embracing this diet can lead to lasting health improvements, making it a valuable choice for those looking to optimise their health.

Impact on Weight Loss

A low-carb, high-protein diet is highly effective for weight loss due to its specific effects on the body's metabolism and hunger regulation mechanisms. Understanding the anatomical and physiological processes behind these effects can help clarify why this dietary approach is so successful.

When you reduce carbohydrate intake, your body uses stored fat as its primary energy source. Typically, the body uses glucose, derived from carbohydrates, for energy. However, when glucose is limited, the body shifts to burning fat through a process called lipolysis. During lipolysis, fat cells break down and release fatty acids into the bloodstream, where they are transported to the liver and converted into ketone bodies. These ketone bodies then serve as an alternative fuel source for the body and brain. This metabolic shift promotes fat loss and helps maintain steady energy levels, reducing the likelihood of energy crashes that can trigger overeating.

High protein intake contributes significantly to weight loss by increasing satiety and reducing appetite. Proteins take longer to digest than carbohydrates, which means they stay in the stomach longer, creating a prolonged feeling of fullness. This extended digestion process helps curb hunger and reduce overall calorie intake. Additionally, proteins stimulate the release of hormones like peptide YY (PYY) and glucagon-like peptide-1 (GLP-1), which signal fullness to the brain and help control appetite.

Another critical aspect of a high-protein, low-carb diet is its impact on thermogenesis, the body's heat production process. Proteins have a higher thermic effect on food (TEF) than fats and carbohydrates, meaning the body uses more energy to digest, absorb, and metabolise protein. This increase in energy expenditure can boost the overall number of calories burned throughout the day, contributing to a more significant calorie deficit and more effective weight loss.

A low-carb, high-protein diet also helps preserve lean muscle mass during weight loss. When the body is in a calorie deficit, it can lose muscle mass and fat. However, protein provides the amino acids necessary for muscle repair and maintenance. Ensuring adequate protein intake supports muscle preservation, crucial for maintaining a healthy metabolism. Muscle tissue burns more calories at rest than fat tissue, so preserving muscle mass helps keep your metabolism active, making it easier to lose weight or maintain weight loss. Furthermore, reducing carbohydrate intake can lead to decreased insulin levels. Insulin is a hormone that regulates blood sugar levels and fat storage. Lower insulin levels reduce the body's tendency to store fat and encourage using stored fat for energy. This hormonal change is particularly beneficial for individuals with insulin resistance or metabolic syndrome, conditions that are often associated with obesity and can hinder weight loss efforts. The impact of a low-carb, high-protein diet on weight loss is multifaceted and scientifically grounded. By promoting fat burning, enhancing satiety, increasing thermogenesis, preserving lean muscle mass, and reducing insulin levels, this dietary approach offers a comprehensive strategy for effective and sustainable weight loss. Embracing these principles can help you achieve your weight loss goals while maintaining overall health and vitality.

Muscle Building

A low-carb, high-protein diet is particularly effective for muscle building because it provides the essential nutrients required for muscle growth and repair while maintaining optimal energy levels. Understanding the physiological processes can clarify why this dietary approach supports muscle development.

Proteins are composed of amino acids, the building blocks of muscle tissue. Tiny tears occur in the muscle fibres when you engage in resistance training or other muscle-building exercises. During recovery, the body repairs these micro-tears, making the muscles more robust and prominent. Adequate protein intake is crucial because it supplies the amino acids necessary for this repair and growth process. The body can only effectively repair muscle tissue with sufficient protein, hindering muscle growth and strength gains.

Leucine, a crucial amino acid, is a critical player in muscle synthesis. It triggers the activation of mTOR (mechanistic target of rapamycin), a complex essential for muscle protein synthesis. A protein-rich diet ensures sufficient leucine and other amino acids, maximising muscle protein synthesis and fostering efficient muscle growth.

Though limited in a high-protein diet, carbohydrates still have a supportive role. Consuming carbs around your workout times aids in replenishing glycogen stores in muscles. Glycogen, the stored form of glucose, is the primary fuel used during high-intensity exercise. By strategically timing carbohydrate intake, you can maintain the energy required for intense workouts without compromising the low-carb nature of your diet. This approach ensures that your muscles have the fuel they need during exercise while relying on protein for repair and growth post-workout.

Another advantage of a high-protein diet is its impact on hormones related to muscle growth. Protein consumption stimulates the release of insulin, an anabolic hormone that helps drive amino acids into muscle cells, promoting muscle growth. A high protein intake can also increase growth hormone and testosterone levels, critical for muscle development. These hormonal changes create an environment that is highly conducive to building muscle.

Adequate hydration and micronutrient intake are also crucial for muscle health. At the same time, protein provides the building blocks for muscle; vitamins and minerals like vitamin D, calcium, and magnesium support muscle function and recovery. Staying well-hydrated helps transport nutrients to muscle cells and aids in the removal of metabolic waste products generated during exercise. It's also worth noting that a high protein, low carb diet can help minimise muscle breakdown during periods of calorie deficit. When trying to lose fat while maintaining muscle mass, consuming enough protein is essential to prevent the body from using muscle tissue as an energy source. This preservation of lean muscle mass is vital for maintaining strength and metabolism during weight loss phases. A low-carb, high-protein diet supports muscle building by providing essential amino acids for muscle repair and growth, optimising hormonal responses, and ensuring adequate energy levels for intense workouts. By understanding and utilising these physiological processes, you can enhance your muscle-building efforts and achieve better results from your training regimen. This dietary approach supports muscle growth and contributes to overall health and well-being, making it a powerful strategy for anyone looking to build and maintain muscle mass.

Testimonials and Success Stories

The accurate measure of any diet's effectiveness lies in the experiences and success stories of those who follow it. A low-carb, high-protein diet has transformed the lives of many, providing numerous health benefits and helping individuals achieve their fitness goals. Here are a few testimonials that highlight the profound impact this dietary approach can have.

Jane, a 35-year-old mother of two, struggled with her weight for years. Despite trying various diets, she struggled to lose weight and maintain her energy levels. After switching to a low-carb, high-protein diet, Jane experienced significant changes. Within the first three months, she lost 20 pounds and noticed a marked improvement in her energy and mood. The carbohydrate reduction helped stabilise her blood sugar levels, preventing the energy crashes she previously experienced. Jane's success story is a testament to how this diet can help manage weight effectively while improving overall well-being.

Mark, a 45-year-old office worker, faced issues with high cholesterol and hypertension. He adopted a low-carb, high-protein diet on his doctor's recommendation. Mark's cholesterol levels improved significantly within six months, with a notable increase in HDL (good cholesterol) and a decrease in LDL (bad cholesterol) and triglycerides. His blood pressure also normalised, reducing his need for medication. Mark attributes his health improvements to the anti-inflammatory effects of lowering carbohydrate intake and the heart-healthy benefits of a higher protein diet.

Sarah, a 28-year-old athlete, used this diet to enhance her performance and recovery. Sarah found that increasing her protein intake supported muscle repair and growth, allowing her to train harder and more frequently. She also noticed quicker recovery times and less muscle soreness after workouts. The diet provided her with sustained energy throughout her training sessions, thanks to the strategic intake of carbs around her workouts. Sarah's experience underscores the benefits of this diet for athletic performance and muscle maintenance.

Michael, a 50-year-old with type 2 diabetes, saw remarkable improvements in his condition after switching to a low-carb, high-protein diet. By reducing his carbohydrate intake, he stabilised his blood sugar levels and reduced his reliance on insulin. Over a year, Michael lost 30 pounds and reported feeling healthier and more energetic than ever. His success story highlights the potential of this diet to manage and even reverse symptoms of type 2 diabetes.

These testimonials demonstrate the diverse benefits of a low-carb, high-protein diet, from weight loss and improved energy levels to better heart health and enhanced athletic performance. By embracing this dietary approach, many have achieved lasting health improvements and a higher quality of life.

CHAPTER 1

How to Store Prepared Foods

Proper storage of prepared foods is essential to maintaining their nutritional value, freshness, and safety. When following a low-carb, high-protein diet, storing your meals correctly is vital to ensure they remain healthy and delicious. Understanding the basic principles of food storage can help you make the most of your meal prep efforts, reduce food waste, and prevent foodborne illnesses.

Refrigeration is one of the most common methods for storing prepared foods. The refrigerator slows the growth of bacteria and mould, which can spoil food and cause illness. To maximise the effectiveness of refrigeration, it's essential to store food at the correct temperature, which should be below 40°F (4°C). Cooked meats, dairy products, and prepared meals should be placed in airtight containers to prevent contamination and preserve moisture. Labelling containers with the date of preparation can help you keep track of freshness and ensure you consume the oldest items first.

Freezing is another effective method for storing prepared foods, especially long-term storage. Freezing food halts the growth of bacteria, yeasts, and moulds by lowering the temperature to 0°F (-18°C) or below. It's crucial to use freezer-safe containers or bags to prevent freezer burn, which can affect the taste and texture of food. When freezing cooked meats, soups, or casseroles, divide them into portions for easier thawing and reheating. Defrosting should be done safely in the refrigerator, microwave, or as part of the cooking process to minimise the risk of bacterial growth.

Weekly meal prep can be a game-changer for those committed to a low-carb, high-protein diet. Dedicating a few hours each week to preparing and portioning meals can save time, reduce stress, and stay on track with your dietary goals. Start by planning your meals and making a comprehensive grocery list. Cook large batches of proteins like chicken, turkey, or fish and complement them with variouslow-carb vegetables. Store these meals in the refrigerator for up to four days or freeze them for more extended storage. Clear, labelled containers can help you quickly identify meals and organise your fridge.

Understanding the science behind food spoilage can also enhance your food storage practices. Bacteria, yeasts, and moulds are the primary culprits of food spoilage. These microorganisms thrive in warm, moist environments, making temperature control essential. Additionally, exposure to air can lead to oxidation, which degrades the quality of fats and oils in food, causing rancidity. By using airtight containers and vacuum-sealing when possible, you can limit exposure to air and extend the shelf life of your meals.

Incorporating proper food storage techniques into your routine ensures the safety and quality of your meals and supports your overall health. For example, fresh vegetables stored correctly retain more vitamins and minerals, contributing to better nutritional intake. Properly stored proteins maintain integrity, ensuring you receive the essential amino acids needed for muscle repair and growth.

Moreover, understanding the impact of different storage methods on food can help you make informed choices. For instance, blanching vegetables before freezing can preserve their colour, texture, and nutritional value. Blanching involves briefly boiling the vegetables and then plunging them into ice water to stop cooking. This technique inactivates enzymes that can cause loss of flavour, colour, and nutrients during storage.

In conclusion, mastering the art of food storage is a vital skill for anyone following a low-carb, high-protein diet. Properly refrigerating, freezing, and preparing your meals can ensure they remain safe, nutritious, and delicious. These practices help you stay on track with your dietary goals and promote overall health and well-being. Whether you're a seasoned meal prepper or new to this approach, implementing these storage techniques will enhance your culinary journey and support a healthier lifestyle.

Techniques for Food Storage

Adequate food storage is a cornerstone of maintaining your meals' quality, safety, and nutritional integrity, especially when adhering to a low-carb, high-protein diet. Proper storage techniques preserve the taste and texture of your food and ensure that you get the maximum health benefits from your dietary choices. Here's a comprehensive guide on using the refrigerator, freezer, and weekly meal prep to optimise food storage. The fridge is one of the most convenient ways to store prepared foods and ingredients. The cold environment of the refrigerator slows down the growth of harmful bacteria and moulds, significantly extending the shelf life of your meals. Your refrigerator should be below 40°F (4°C) for optimal results—store meats and dairy products in airtight containers to prevent contamination and dehydration. Properly sealed containers also avoid cross-contamination from raw to cooked foods. Vegetables should be stored in the crisper drawer, which maintains a slightly higher humidity level, preserving their freshness longer. Eggs, a staple in high-protein diets, should be stored in their original carton to keep them from absorbing strong odours from other foods.

The freezer is an invaluable tool for long-term food storage. Freezing halts the growth of bacteria and other pathogens by keeping the temperature at 0°F (-18°C) or lower. When freezing food, it's crucial to use appropriate containers or freezer bags to prevent freezer burn, which can compromise the quality and flavour of the food. Dividing meals into individual portions before freezing can save time and reduce waste. For example, freeze chicken breasts, steaks, or fish fillets on a baking sheet before transferring them to a freezer bag. This method ensures they don't stick together, allowing you to defrost only what you need. Labelling containers with the date of freezing helps track the age of the food and ensures you use the oldest items first.

Weekly meal prep is an excellent strategy for those following a structured diet. By dedicating a few hours each week to cooking and portioning meals, you can ensure that you always have healthy options readily available. Start with a meal plan that outlines your weekly meals, providing a balance of protein, healthy fats, and low-carb vegetables. Cook large batches of food, such as grilled chicken, roasted vegetables, and quinoa, and divide them into individual servings. Store these meals in clear, labelled containers to keep your refrigerator organised and make it easy to grab meals on the go. Incorporate a variety of seasonings and cooking methods to keep your meals exciting and prevent flavour fatigue.

Understanding the anatomical processes related to food storage can enhance your approach. For instance, when proteins are stored improperly, they can degrade and lose their essential amino acids, crucial for muscle repair and growth. Proper storage ensures you get the full nutritional benefit from your food, supporting your overall health and fitness goals. Additionally, keeping vegetables fresh and crisp retains their fibre content, which aids in digestion and helps maintain steady blood sugar levels.

Another tip for adequate food storage is to cool food before refrigerating or freezing it. Placing hot food directly into the fridge or freezer can raise the internal temperature, putting other foods at risk and creating an environment where bacteria can thrive. Allowing food to cool to room temperature before storing it helps maintain the safety and efficiency of your storage environment.

Mastering food storage techniques is essential for anyone committed to a low-carb, high-protein diet. You can ensure your meals remain fresh, nutritious, and safe by effectively utilising your refrigerator and freezer and implementing a consistent meal prep routine. These practices help you adhere to your dietary goals and promote better overall health by preserving your food's quality and nutrient content. Embracing these storage techniques will enhance your dietary journey and support a healthier, more organised lifestyle.

CHAPTER 2

Cooking Tips and Basic Techniques

One of the fundamental aspects of cooking high-protein meals is to avoid overcooking, which can lead to the denaturation of proteins. Denaturation is when proteins lose their structure due to heat, affecting their nutritional quality. For example, overcooking chicken or fish can make them tough and dry, reducing their palatability. Using a food thermometer can help ensure that meats are cooked to a safe internal temperature without being overdone. For chicken, the safe internal temperature is 165°F (74°C), while for beef and fish, it is 145°F (63°C).

Marinating is an excellent technique to enhance the flavour of your proteins without adding extra carbs. A simple marinade can be made using olive oil, lemon juice, garlic, and herbs. Marinating meat adds flavour and helps tenderise it, making it more enjoyable. Additionally, acidic components in marinades, such as vinegar or citrus juice, can help break down proteins, making them easier to digest and absorb.

Steaming and blanching are cooking methods that preserve the nutrients in vegetables, which are vital to a low-carb diet. Steaming involves cooking vegetables in steam over boiling water, which helps retain water-soluble vitamins like C and B. Blanching involves briefly boiling vegetables and then plunging them into ice water to stop the cooking process. This method preserves vegetables' vibrant colour and crisp texture while maintaining their nutritional value.

Stir-frying is another effective technique for cooking low-carb, high-protein meals. This method involves quickly cooking small pieces of food over high heat in a small amount of oil. Stir-frying helps to preserve the texture and nutrients of both proteins and vegetables. You can create delicious and nutritious meals in minutes using a wok or a large skillet. Be sure to use oils with high smoke points, such as avocado or coconut oil, to avoid the formation of harmful compounds during cooking.

Understanding the importance of portion control is also crucial in a low-carb, high-protein diet. Using a kitchen scale to measure portions of meat, fish, and vegetables ensures you consume the appropriate amounts of each nutrient. This practice helps you stay within your dietary goals and prevents overeating. For instance, the standard portion size for meat or fish is about 3-4 ounces, roughly the size of a deck of cards.

Incorporating herbs and spices into your cooking enhances flavour and provides additional health benefits. Herbs like basil, rosemary, and thyme contain antioxidants that can reduce inflammation and support overall health. Spices such as turmeric and ginger have anti-inflammatory properties and can aid digestion. Experimenting with different herbs and spices can make your meals more exciting and enjoyable while adding a nutritional boost.

Using proper cooking techniques can also reduce the formation of harmful substances. For example, cooking meats at very high temperatures, such as grilling or frying, can produce advanced glycation end products (AGEs) and heterocyclic amines (HCAs) linked to chronic diseases. Use gentler cooking methods like baking, steaming, or sous-vide to minimise these risks.

In conclusion, mastering basic cooking techniques is essential for anyone committed to a low-carb, high-protein diet. You can create delicious, nutritious meals that support your health goals by avoiding overcooking, using methods that preserve nutrients, controlling portions, and incorporating healthy herbs and spices. These skills enhance the quality of your food and ensure that you maximise the health benefits of your dietary choices.

Essential Kitchen Tools

Proper kitchen tools are fundamental for anyone following a low-carb, high-protein diet. These tools make meal preparation more accessible and help maintain the nutritional quality of your food. Equipped with the proper utensils and appliances, you can streamline your cooking process and ensure your meals are delicious and healthy.

A high-quality chef's knife is indispensable. This versatile tool allows precise cutting, chopping, and slicing, which is crucial for preparing ingredients like vegetables and meats. A sharp knife speeds up your prep time and ensures you can cut through proteins cleanly without tearing the fibres, preserving their texture and nutritional integrity. Properly cut vegetables retain more nutrients and cook more evenly, contributing to the overall healthiness of your meals.

Cutting boards are another essential item. It's advisable to have multiple cutting boards to avoid cross-contamination between raw meats and vegetables. Plastic cutting boards are easy to sanitise, making them ideal for beef, while wooden boards are excellent for vegetables and other dry ingredients. Keeping your cutting boards clean and well-maintained prevents the growth of bacteria that could potentially contaminate your food.

A set of measuring cups and spoons is crucial for anyone serious about maintaining a balanced diet. Accurate measurements ensure that you adhere to portion sizes, particularly important in a high-protein, low-carb diet where balance is critical. Measuring tools help you track your macronutrient intake, ensuring you get enough protein without over-consuming carbohydrates.

A food scale is another valuable tool. Weighing your food allows for precise portion control, ensuring you consume the correct amount of protein and carbohydrates per meal. This is especially important for those monitoring their weight loss or muscle-building intake. Consistent portion sizes help maintain stable blood sugar levels and support metabolic health.

Investing in quality cookware, such as non-stick pans and stainless-steel pots, can significantly improve your cooking experience. Non-stick pans require less oil, helping you prepare low-fat meals that align with your dietary goals. Stainless steel pots are durable and versatile, suitable for boiling, steaming, and making soups, which are excellent for a high-protein diet.

Blenders and food processors are invaluable for creating smoothies, protein shakes, and pureeing vegetables for soups and sauces. These appliances can quickly break down whole foods into easily digestible forms, preserving their nutrients. Blending protein shakes, for instance, allows you to combine various ingredients like fruits, vegetables, and protein powder into a nutritious meal that supports muscle recovery and growth.

An instant-read thermometer ensures your proteins are cooked to safe temperatures. This tool helps prevent overcooking, preserving the tenderness and moisture of meats. Properly cooked proteins are not only safer to eat but also retain more of their nutritional value.

A slow or pressure cooker can simplify meal prep and save time. These appliances are perfect for preparing large batches of protein-rich meals like stews, soups, and roasts. Slow cooking at low temperatures helps preserve the integrity of amino acids in proteins, ensuring you get the full nutritional benefit.

Spice grinders and herb scissors are great for adding flavour without extra calories. Freshly ground spices and finely chopped herbs enhance the taste of your dishes while providing additional health benefits. Many herbs and spices contain antioxidants and anti-inflammatory compounds that support overall health.

Food storage containers are essential for keeping your prepped meals fresh and organised. Glass containers are preferable as they are microwave-safe and do not leach chemicals into your food. Proper storage helps maintain the nutritional quality of your meals and makes it easier to follow your diet consistently. Equipping your kitchen with the right tools can significantly enhance your cooking experience and support your dietary goals. From precise measuring and cutting to efficient cooking and storing, these essential kitchen tools ensure that your low-carb, high-protein meals are prepared safely, efficiently, and nutritiously. By investing in quality tools, you can make healthy cooking an enjoyable and sustainable part of your lifestyle.

Techniques for Cutting and Preparing Ingredients

Mastering the techniques for cutting and preparing ingredients is essential for anyone committed to a low-carb, high-protein diet. These skills ensure that your meals are nutritious, visually appealing, and delicious. Proper preparation techniques help retain the nutritional value of ingredients, which is crucial for maintaining a healthy diet.

Understanding how to cut vegetables correctly is fundamental. Different vegetables require different cutting techniques to maximise their flavour and nutritional value. For instance, chopping leafy greens like spinach or kale into thin strips (a method known as chiffonade) helps preserve their vitamins and minerals while making them easier to incorporate into dishes. When cutting cruciferous vegetables like broccoli or cauliflower, using a sharp knife to separate the florets ensures minimal nutrient loss and maintains their crunchy texture.

Dicing and julienning are two standard cutting techniques that can enhance the presentation and texture of your dishes. Dicing involves cutting vegetables or proteins into small, even cubes, which allows for uniform cooking and easy flavour blending. On the other hand, Julienning involves cutting ingredients into thin, matchstick-like strips, which can add a pleasing texture to salads and stir-fries. These techniques ensure that your meals cook evenly and look professionally prepared.

Understanding the grain of the meat is crucial for proteins. Cutting against the grain, or the direction the muscle fibres run ensures the meat is tender and more accessible to chew. This technique is essential for tougher cuts of meat, such as flank steak or brisket. Slicing meat thinly also helps with portion control, which is beneficial for maintaining a balanced diet.

Marinating proteins before cooking can enhance flavour and tenderness. Marinating typically involves soaking the meat in acids (like vinegar or lemon juice), oils, and herbs. The acids in the marinade help break down the muscle fibres, making the meat more tender. The oil and herbs also add flavour without adding carbs, making your high-protein meals more enjoyable.

Marinating meats for an adequate amount of time – usually a few hours or overnight – is essential to allow the flavoursto penetrate fully.

Blanching is another helpful technique, especially for preparing vegetables. Blanching involves briefly boiling vegetables and then plunging them into ice water to stop cooking. This technique helps preserve vegetables' colour, texture, and nutritional value. Blanching is particularly effective for green beans, asparagus, and broccoli, which can lose their vibrancy and nutrients if overcooked.

Proper preparation also involves ensuring that ingredients are clean and safe to eat. Washing vegetables thoroughly removes dirt, bacteria, and pesticides. A salad spinner can effectively dry leafy greens after washing, ensuring they are ready for salads or cooking. When dealing with proteins, it's essential to use separate cutting boards for raw meats and vegetables to avoid cross-contamination.

Using a mandoline slicer can be a game-changer for preparing vegetables uniformly. A mandoline lets you slice vegetables thinly and evenly, which is great for making dishes like zucchini noodles or thinly sliced salads. Uniform slices look appealing and cook evenly, ensuring consistent texture and flavour throughout the dish.Another critical aspect of preparation is the mise en place, a French term meaning "everything in its place." This technique involves preparing and organising all your ingredients before you start cooking. By having all ingredients measured, chopped, and ready to go, you can streamline the cooking process, making it more efficient and enjoyable. This method also ensures that you don't miss any steps in a recipe, leading to better results.Understanding and applying these techniques can make your cooking process more efficient and enjoyable, ultimately supporting your health and dietary goals.

Tips for Efficient and Clean Cooking

Efficient and clean cooking is essential for anyone following a low-carb, high-protein diet. Not only does it save time and reduce stress, but it also ensures that your meals are prepared hygienically, maximising their nutritional benefits. Here are some expert tips to help you achieve efficiency and cleanliness in the kitchen.

Using a kitchen timer can significantly enhance your cooking efficiency. Timers help you keep track of cooking times, ensuring that your food is cooked perfectly without constant monitoring. This allows you to multitask, such as preparing other ingredients or cleaning up as you go. For example, while baking your chicken, you can chop vegetables or wash dishes, making the most of your time.

Cleaning as you go is a crucial habit for maintaining a tidy and efficient kitchen. Instead of letting dirty dishes and utensils pile up, wash them immediately after use. This practice prevents clutter and makes the final cleanup much more manageable. Keeping a sink filled with hot, soapy water lets you quickly clean items as you finish them. Wiping countertops and cutting boards regularly during cooking helps maintain a clean workspace.

Using high-quality, non-stick cookware can make cooking and cleaning much more efficient. Non-stick surfaces reduce the need for excessive oil, making your meals healthier and more accessible. They simplify cleanup, as food residue is less likely to stick to the pan. Investing in durable, easy-to-clean kitchen tools can save you time and effort in the long run.

Multitasking is a skill that can significantly enhance cooking efficiency. For example, you can marinate your proteins while chopping vegetables or prepare side dishes while the main course is cooking. By coordinating tasks, you can ensure that all meal components are ready simultaneously, reducing cooking time. However, it's essential to stay organised and focused to avoid mistakes.

Another essential tip for efficient cooking is maintaining sharp knives. Dull blades can slow your prep work and increase the risk of injury. Regularly sharpening your knives ensures you can cut through ingredients quickly and safely, making meal preparation more efficient. Proper knife care also prolongs the life of your blades, saving you money in the long run.

Using parchment paper or silicone baking mats can make baking and roasting more efficient and less messy. These tools prevent food from sticking to baking sheets, reducing the need for scrubbing and soaking. They also ensure even cooking and browning, enhancing the quality of your meals.

Labelling and dating your stored food is essential for efficient meal management. Clear labels help you quickly identify the contents of containers, saving time when you're ready to eat. Dating your food ensures that you consume items in the correct order, reducing waste and ensuring that your meals are always fresh.

Efficient and clean cooking is integral to maintaining a low-carb, high-protein diet. By planning and organizing your workspace, using high-quality tools, and adopting intelligent cooking habits, you can streamline your meal preparation and maintain a hygienic kitchen. These practices save time and effort and ensure that your meals are nutritious and enjoyable, supporting your overall health and dietary goals.

CHAPTER 3
- RENEWED ENERGY: POWERFUL RECIPES FOR RECOVERY

Curry Chicken with Broccoli and Brown Rice

- **Preparation time (P.T.):** 30 minutes

- **Ingredients (Ingr.):**

  o 300 g chicken breasts, cubed

  o 15 ml olive oil

  o 150 g onion, diced

  o 10 g garlic, minced

  o 10 g curry powder

  o 400 ml coconut milk

  o 200 g broccoli florets

  o 180 g brown rice

  o Salt and pepper to taste

- **Servings (Serves):** 2

- **Mode of cooking:** Stovetop

- **Procedure:**

1. Prepare the brown rice per the directions on the package.

2. In a large pan over medium heat, warm the olive oil. Add the garlic and onion, and cook until transparent.

3. Cook the cubed chicken until it turns golden brown on all sides.

4. Add the curry powder and simmer for an additional one minute.

5. Add the coconut milk, boil, and then add the broccoli florets.

6. Simmer until the chicken is cooked through and the broccoli is soft, about 10 minutes.

7. Season to taste with salt and pepper.

8. Spoon the chicken curry onto brown rice.

- **Nutritional values:**

  o Calories: 450 kcal

  o Protein: 35 g

  o Carbohydrates: 50 g

  o Fat: 15 g

Baked Salmon with Asparagus and Quinoa

- **Preparation time (P.T.):** 25 minutes

- **Ingredients (Ingr.):**

  o 2 salmon fillets (approximately 200 g each)

- o 15 ml olive oil

- o 1 lemon, sliced

- o 450 g asparagus, trimmed

- o 180 g quinoa

- o 500 ml vegetable broth

- o Salt and pepper to taste

- **Servings (Serves):** 2

- **Mode of cooking:** Oven and stovetop

- **Procedure:**

1.Set oven temperature to 200°C/400°F.

2. Arrange the salmon fillets on a baking sheet, cover with lemon slices, and drizzle with olive oil. Add pepper and salt for seasoning.

3. Encircle the fish with asparagus and bake for 15 minutes, or until the salmon is cooked through.

4. Prepare the quinoa per the directions on the package while the salmon bakes.

5. Arrange the asparagus and cooked salmon on top of quinoa.

- **Nutritional values:**

- o Calories: 500 kcal

- o Protein: 40 g

- o Carbohydrates: 30 g

- o Fat: 20 g

Turkey and Avocado Salad

- **Preparation time (P.T.):** 15 minutes

- **Ingredients (Ingr.):**

- o 300 g cooked turkey breast, diced

- o 1 avocado, diced (approximately 150 g)

- o 150 g cherry tomatoes, halved

- o 100 g cucumber, diced

- o 200 g mixed greens

- o 60 g feta cheese, crumbled

- o 30 ml olive oil

- o 15 ml balsamic vinegar

- o Salt and pepper to taste

- **Servings (Serves):** 2

- **Mode of cooking:** No cooking required

- **Procedure:**

1. In a large bowl, combine turkey, avocado, cherry tomatoes, cucumber, and mixed greens.

2. Sprinkle feta cheese on top.

3. In a small bowl, whisk together olive oil and balsamic vinegar. Season with salt and pepper.

4. Drizzle the dressing over the salad and toss to combine.

- **Nutritional values:**
    - Calories: 350 kcal
    - Protein: 30 g
    - Carbohydrates: 20 g
    - Fat: 20 g

Scrambled Eggs with Spinach and Tomatoes

- **Preparation time (P.T.):** 10 minutes
- **Ingredients (Ingr.):**
    - 4 eggs (approximately 200 g)
    - 15 ml olive oil
    - 100 g spinach, washed and chopped
    - 100 g cherry tomatoes, halved
    - Salt and pepper to taste
- **Servings (Serves):** 2
- **Mode of cooking:** Stovetop
- **Procedure:**

1. Beat the eggs in a bowl with a dash of pepper and salt.

2. In a pan over medium heat, preheat the olive oil.

3. Include the cherry tomatoes and spinach, and sauté until the tomatoes are slightly softened and the spinach has wilted.

4. Add the eggs to the pan and heat, stirring constantly, until the eggs are fully cooked and scrambled.

5. Present right away.

- **Nutritional values:**
    - Calories: 250 kcal
    - Protein: 20 g
    - Carbohydrates: 5 g
    - Fat: 18 g

Banana and Peanut Butter Protein Smoothie

- **Preparation time (P.T.):** 5 minutes

- **Ingredients (Ingr.):**

  - 1 banana (approximately 120 g)

  - 30 g peanut butter

  - 30 g protein powder

  - 250 ml almond milk

  - 1 tsp honey (optional)

- **Servings (Serves):** 1

- **Mode of cooking:** Blender

- **Procedure:**

1. Fill a blender with all the ingredients.

2. Purée until silky.

3. Transfer into a glass and serve right away.

- **Nutritional values:**

  - Calories: 350 kcal

  - Protein: 25 g

  - Carbohydrates: 30 g

  - Fat: 15 g

Grilled Steak with Mixed Vegetables

- **Preparation time (P.T.):** 20 minutes

- **Ingredients (Ingr.):**

  - 300 g beef steak

  - 15 ml olive oil

  - 1 bell pepper, sliced (approximately 150 g)

  - 1 zucchini, sliced (approximately 200 g)

  - 1 red onion, sliced (approximately 100 g)

  - Salt and pepper to taste

- **Servings (Serves):** 2

- **Mode of cooking:** Grill and stovetop

- **Procedure:**

1. Turn the heat up to medium-high on the grill.

2. Season steak with salt and pepper after brushing it with olive oil.

3. Grill the steak until the desired level of doneness, about 5 to 7 minutes per side.

4. Heat the leftover olive oil in a pan over medium heat.

5. Include the red onion, zucchini, and bell pepper. Vegetables should be sautéed until soft and beginning to brown.

6. Present the steak with a mixture of veggies.

- **Nutritional values:**

  - Calories: 450 kcal

  - Protein: 35 g

  - Carbohydrates: 10 g

  - Fat: 30 g

Quinoa and Lean Meat Stuffed Peppers

- **Preparation time (P.T.):** 35 minutes

- **Ingredients (Ingr.):**

  - 4 bell peppers (approximately 600 g)

  - 200 g lean ground beef or turkey

  - 150 g cooked quinoa

  - 100 g onion, diced

  - 2 cloves garlic, minced (10 g)

  - 400 g diced tomatoes (canned)

  - 30 g tomato paste

  - 15 ml olive oil

  - 1 tsp dried oregano (2 g)

  - Salt and pepper to taste

- **Servings (Serves):** 4

- **Mode of cooking:** Oven and stovetop

- **Procedure:**

1. Set oven temperature to 190°C/375°F.

2. Slice off the bell peppers' tops and take out the seeds.

3. In a pan over medium heat, preheat the olive oil. Add the garlic and onion, and cook until transparent.

4. Cook the ground meat until it turns brown. Add the quinoa, tomato paste, diced tomatoes, oregano, salt, and pepper. Simmer for five minutes.

5. Stuff the meat and quinoa mixture into each bell pepper.

6. Transfer the filled peppers to an ovenproof tray and secure with foil.

7. Do a 25-minute bake.

- **Nutritional values:**

  - Calories: 300 kcal

  - Protein: 25 g

  - Carbohydrates: 30 g

  - Fat: 10 g

Swordfish Fillet with Grilled Zucchini

- **Preparation time (P.T.):** 20 minutes

- **Ingredients (Ingr.):**

  - 2 swordfish fillets (approximately 200 g each)

  - 20 ml olive oil

  - 1 lemon, sliced

  - 2 zucchinis, sliced (approximately 400 g)

  - Salt and pepper to taste

- **Servings (Serves):** 2

- **Mode of cooking:** Grill

- **Procedure:**

1. Turn the grill's heat up to medium-high.

2. Season swordfish fillets with salt and pepper after brushing them with olive oil. Add slices of lemon on top.

3. Drizzle slices of zucchini with olive oil and sprinkle with salt and pepper.

4. Swordfish fillets should be cooked through after grilling for five to six minutes on each side.

5. Grill the zucchini slices until they are soft and have a hint of char, two to three minutes on each side.

6. Serve the grilled zucchini beside the swordfish fillets.

- **Nutritional values:**

  - Calories: 400 kcal

  - Protein: 35 g

  - Carbohydrates: 10 g

  - Fat: 25 g

Turkey Meatballs with Cucumber Salad

- **Preparation time (P.T.):** 30 minutes

- **Ingredients (Ingr.):**

  - 300 g ground turkey

  - 1 egg (50 g)

  - 50 g breadcrumbs

- 1 clove garlic, minced (5 g)
- 30 g Parmesan cheese, grated
- 15 ml olive oil
- 1 cucumber, thinly sliced (approximately 200 g)
- 100 g cherry tomatoes, halved
- 50 g red onion, thinly sliced
- 30 ml apple cider vinegar
- Salt and pepper to taste

- **Servings (Serves):** 2
- **Mode of cooking:** Oven and stovetop
- **Procedure:**

1. Set oven temperature to 190°C/375°F.

2. Combine the ground turkey, egg, breadcrumbs, Parmesan cheese, garlic, salt, and pepper in a bowl. Stir thoroughly and shape into meatballs.

3. In a pan over medium heat, preheat the olive oil. After the meatballs are browned on all sides, place them on a baking sheet.

4. Bake the meatballs for 15 minutes, or until they are thoroughly cooked.

5. Combine cucumber, red onion, and cherry tomatoes in a bowl. Add salt, pepper, and apple cider vinegar and toss.

6. Present cucumber salad alongside turkey meatballs.

- **Nutritional values:**

- Calories: 350 kcal
- Protein: 30 g
- Carbohydrates: 20 g
- Fat: 15 g

Egg White Omelet with Mushrooms and Onions

- **Preparation time (P.T.):** 15 minutes

- **Ingredients (Ingr.):**

- 6 egg whites (approximately 200 g)
- 150 g mushrooms, sliced
- 100 g onion, diced
- 15 ml olive oil
- Salt and pepper to taste

- **Servings (Serves):** 2
- **Mode of cooking:** Stovetop

- **Procedure:**

1. Beat egg whites in a bowl with a dash of pepper and salt.

2. In a pan over medium heat, preheat the olive oil. Sauté the onions until they become transparent.

3. Cook the mushrooms until they are tender.

4. Pour the egg whites into the pan and simmer until the eggs set, stirring from time to time.

5. Present right away.

- **Nutritional values:**
  - Calories: 200 kcal
  - Protein: 20 g
  - Carbohydrates: 10 g
  - Fat: 10 g

Chicken Salad with Chia Seeds

- **Preparation time (P.T.):** 15 minutes
- **Ingredients (Ingr.):**
  - 200 g cooked chicken breast, shredded
  - 50 g mixed greens
  - 1 avocado, diced (approximately 150 g)
  - 100 g cherry tomatoes, halved
  - 1 cucumber, diced (approximately 150 g)
  - 20 g chia seeds
  - 30 ml olive oil
  - 15 ml lemon juice
  - Salt and pepper to taste
- **Servings (Serves):** 2
- **Mode of cooking:** No cooking required
- **Procedure:**

1. Put the chicken, cucumber, cherry tomatoes, avocado, mixed greens, and avocado in a big bowl.

2. Add a few chia seeds to the top.

3. Combine the lemon juice and olive oil in a small bowl. Add pepper and salt for seasoning.

4. Pour the salad with the dressing and toss to mix.

- **Nutritional values:**
  - Calories: 350 kcal
  - Protein: 30 g

- ○ Carbohydrates: 15 g

- ○ Fat: 20 g

Strawberry Mint Protein Smoothie

- **Preparation time (P.T.):** 5 minutes

- **Ingredients (Ingr.):**

  - ○ 150 g strawberries, hulled

  - ○ 30 g protein powder

  - ○ 250 ml almond milk

  - ○ 10 mint leaves

  - ○ 1 tsp honey (optional)

- **Servings (Serves):** 1

- **Mode of cooking:** Blender

- **Procedure:**

1. Fill a blender with all the ingredients.

2. Purée until silky.

3. Transfer into a glass and serve right away.

- **Nutritional values:**

  - ○ Calories: 200 kcal

  - ○ Protein: 20 g

  - ○ Carbohydrates: 20 g

  - ○ Fat: 5 g

Almond-Crusted Cod with Broccoli

- **Preparation time (P.T.):** 25 minutes

- **Ingredients (Ingr.):**

  - ○ 2 cod fillets (approximately 200 g each)

  - ○ 50 g ground almonds

  - ○ 1 egg, beaten (50 g)

  - ○ 30 ml olive oil

  - ○ 300 g broccoli florets

  - ○ Salt and pepper to taste

- **Servings (Serves):** 2

- **Mode of cooking:** Oven and stovetop

- **Procedure:**

1. Set oven temperature to 190°C/375°F.

2. Coat the fish fillets with ground almonds after dipping them in the beaten egg.

3. In a pan over medium heat, preheat the olive oil. Brown all sides of the fish fillets.

4. After moving the cod to a baking sheet, bake it for ten minutes, or until it is well done.

5. Cook broccoli in steam until soft.

6. Present cod coated in almonds alongside steaming broccoli.

- **Nutritional values:**

  o Calories: 350 kcal

  o Protein: 30 g

  o Carbohydrates: 10 g

  o Fat: 20 g

Grilled Chicken with Lemon Herb Sauce

- **Preparation time (P.T.):** 20 minutes

- **Ingredients (Ingr.):**

  o 2 chicken breasts (approximately 300 g)

  o 30 ml olive oil

  o 1 lemon, juiced

  o 1 tsp dried thyme (2 g)

  o 1 tsp dried rosemary (2 g)

  o Salt and pepper to taste

- **Servings (Serves):** 2

- **Mode of cooking:** Grill

- **Procedure:**

1. Turn the grill's heat up to medium-high.

2. Combine the olive oil, lemon juice, rosemary, thyme, salt, and pepper in a small bowl.

3. Grill the chicken breasts for 7 to 8 minutes on each side, or until they are cooked through, after brushing them with the mixture.

4. Serve right away.

- **Nutritional values:**

  o Calories: 300 kcal

  o Protein: 35 g

  o Carbohydrates: 5 g

  o Fat: 15 g

Egg White Frittata with Bell Peppers and Red Onions

- **Preparation time (P.T.):** 15 minutes

- **Ingredients (Ingr.):**

  o 6 egg whites (approximately 200 g)

  o 1 bell pepper, diced (approximately 150 g)

o 100 g red onion, diced

o 15 ml olive oil

o Salt and pepper to taste

- **Servings (Serves):** 2

- **Mode of cooking:** Stovetop

- **Procedure:**

1. Beat egg whites in a bowl with a dash of pepper and salt.

2. In a pan over medium heat, preheat the olive oil. Add the red onion and bell pepper, and cook until tender.

3. Add the egg whites to the pan and simmer, stirring periodically, until set.

4. Serve right away.

- **Nutritional values:**

o Calories: 150 kcal

o Protein: 20 g

o Carbohydrates: 10 g

o Fat: 5 g

Kale Salad with Smoked Salmon

- **Preparation time (P.T.):** 15 minutes

- **Ingredients (Ingr.):**

o 150 g smoked salmon, sliced

o 200 g kale, chopped

o 1 avocado, diced (approximately 150 g)

o 100 g cherry tomatoes, halved

o 30 g red onion, thinly sliced

o 30 ml olive oil

o 15 ml lemon juice

o Salt and pepper to taste

- **Servings (Serves):** 2

- **Mode of cooking:** No cooking required

- **Procedure:**

1. Put the kale, avocado, cherry tomatoes, and red onion in a big bowl.

2. Place slices of smoked salmon on top.

3. Combine the lemon juice and olive oil in a small bowl. Add pepper and salt for seasoning.

4. Pour the salad with the dressing and toss to mix.

- **Nutritional values:**

o Calories: 350 kcal

o Protein: 20 g

o Carbohydrates: 15 g

o Fat: 25 g

Oven-Roasted Chicken with Sweet Potatoes and Rosemary

- **Preparation time (P.T.):** 40 minutes

- **Ingredients (Ingr.):**

  - 2 chicken thighs (approximately 300 g)

  - 400 g sweet potatoes, diced

  - 30 ml olive oil

  - 2 sprigs fresh rosemary

  - 1 tsp garlic powder (5 g)

  - Salt and pepper to taste

- **Servings (Serves):** 2

- **Mode of cooking:** Oven

- **Procedure:**

1. Set oven temperature to 200°C/400°F.

2. Combine sweet potatoes, olive oil, garlic powder, rosemary, salt, and pepper in a baking dish.

3. Top the sweet potatoes with the chicken thighs, then sprinkle with salt and pepper.

4. Bake for 35 to 40 minutes, or until the sweet potatoes are soft and the chicken is thoroughly cooked.

5. Present right away.

- **Nutritional values:**

  - Calories: 500 kcal

  - Protein: 30 g

  - Carbohydrates: 45 g

  - Fat: 20 g

Chocolate Raspberry Protein Smoothie

- **Preparation time (P.T.):** 5 minutes

- **Ingredients (Ingr.):**

  - 150 g raspberries

  - 30 g chocolate protein powder

  - 250 ml almond milk

  - 1 tsp honey (optional)

- **Servings (Serves):** 1

- **Mode of cooking:** Blender

- **Procedure:**

1. Fill a blender with all the ingredients.

2. Purée until silky.

3. Transfer into a glass and serve right away.

- **Nutritional values:**
  - Calories: 200 kcal
  - Protein: 20 g
  - Carbohydrates: 25 g
  - Fat: 5 g

Grilled Tuna with Green Bean Salad

- **Preparation time (P.T.):** 20 minutes
- **Ingredients (Ingr.):**
  - 2 tuna steaks (approximately 200 g each)
  - 200 g green beans, trimmed
  - 100 g cherry tomatoes, halved
  - 30 g red onion, thinly sliced
  - 30 ml olive oil
  - 15 ml balsamic vinegar
  - Salt and pepper to taste
- **Servings (Serves):** 2
- **Mode of cooking:** Grill and stovetop
- **Procedure:**

1. Turn the grill's heat up to medium-high.

2. Season tuna steaks with salt and pepper after brushing them with olive oil. Grill for desired doneness, about 3–4 minutes per side.

3. Heat the leftover olive oil in a pan over medium heat. Cook the green beans until they become soft.

4. Put the red onion, cherry tomatoes, and green beans in a bowl. Add salt, pepper, and balsamic vinegar and toss.

5. Present green bean salad beside grilled tuna.

- **Nutritional values:**
  - Calories: 350 kcal
  - Protein: 35 g
  - Carbohydrates: 10 g
  - Fat: 20 g

Chicken with Honey Mustard Sauce

- **Preparation time (P.T.):** 25 minutes
- **Ingredients (Ingr.):**
  - 2 chicken breasts (approximately 300 g)

- o 30 ml olive oil

- o 30 ml honey

- o 30 ml Dijon mustard

- o 1 tsp garlic powder (5 g)

- o Salt and pepper to taste

- **Servings (Serves):** 2

- **Mode of cooking:** Stovetop

- **Procedure:**

1.Combine the honey, Dijon mustard, garlic powder, salt, and pepper in a small bowl.

2. In a pan over medium heat, preheat the olive oil. When the chicken breasts are cooked on both sides, add them and simmer.

3. After adding the honey mustard sauce, simmer the chicken for a further five to seven minutes, or until it is thoroughly cooked.

4. Serve right away.

- **Nutritional values:**

- o Calories: 300 kcal

- o Protein: 35 g

- o Carbohydrates: 10 g

- o Fat: 10 g

Spinach and Feta Omelet

- **Preparation time (P.T.):** 15 minutes

- **Ingredients (Ingr.):**

- o 4 eggs (approximately 200 g)

- o 100 g spinach, washed and chopped

- o 50 g feta cheese, crumbled

- o 15 ml olive oil

- o Salt and pepper to taste

- **Servings (Serves):** 2

- **Mode of cooking:** Stovetop

- **Procedure:**

1. Beat the eggs in a bowl with a dash of pepper and salt.

2. In a pan over medium heat, preheat the olive oil. When the spinach begins to wilt, add it.

3. Add the eggs to the pan and cook them until they set. Spoon one half of the omelet with feta cheese, then fold the other half over the cheese.

4. Serve right away.

- **Nutritional values:**
  - Calories: 250 kcal
  - Protein: 20 g
  - Carbohydrates: 5 g
  - Fat: 18 g

Sesame-Crusted Salmon with Stir-Fried Vegetables

- **Preparation time (P.T.):** 25 minutes

- **Ingredients (Ingr.):**
  - 2 salmon fillets (approximately 200 g each)
  - 30 g sesame seeds
  - 15 ml olive oil
  - 1 bell pepper, sliced (approximately 150 g)
  - 1 carrot, julienned (approximately 100 g)
  - 100 g snap peas
  - 2 cloves garlic, minced (10 g)
  - 30 ml soy sauce
  - 15 ml rice vinegar
  - 1 tsp ginger, grated (5 g)
  - Salt and pepper to taste

- **Servings (Serves):** 2
- **Mode of cooking:** Stovetop
- **Procedure:**

1. Apply sesame seeds to the fillets of salmon.

2. In a pan over medium heat, preheat the olive oil. Salmon fillets should be cooked through after 5 to 6 minutes on each side.

3. Heat the leftover olive oil in a different pan over medium heat. Add the ginger and garlic, and cook until aromatic.

4. Include the snap peas, carrot, and bell pepper. Sauté the veggies until they are crisp-tender.

5. Add rice vinegar and soy sauce and stir. Simmer for an additional two minutes.

6. Serve stir-fried veggies beside salmon coated in sesame.

- **Nutritional values:**
  - Calories: 450 kcal
  - Protein: 35 g
  - Carbohydrates: 15 g
  - Fat: 25 g

Coffee and Cocoa Protein Smoothie

- **Preparation time (P.T.):** 5 minutes

- **Ingredients (Ingr.):**

    o 1 banana (approximately 120 g)

    o 30 g chocolate protein powder

    o 250 ml cold brewed coffee

    o 1 tsp cocoa powder (optional)

    o 1 tsp honey (optional)

- **Servings (Serves):** 1

- **Mode of cooking:** Blender

- **Procedure:**

1. Fill a blender with all the ingredients.

2. Purée until silky.

3. Transfer into a glass and serve right away.

- **Nutritional values:**

    o Calories: 200 kcal

    o Protein: 20 g

    o Carbohydrates: 25 g

    o Fat: 5 g

Turkey Salad with Walnuts and Blueberries

- **Preparation time (P.T.):** 15 minutes

- **Ingredients (Ingr.):**

    o 200 g cooked turkey breast, sliced

    o 50 g mixed greens

    o 50 g walnuts, chopped

    o 100 g blueberries

    o 1 apple, sliced (approximately 150 g)

    o 30 ml olive oil

    o 15 ml balsamic vinegar

    o Salt and pepper to taste

- **Servings (Serves):** 2

- **Mode of cooking:** No cooking required

- **Procedure:**

1. Combine the turkey, apple slices, walnuts, blueberries, and mixed greens in a big bowl.

2. Combine the olive oil and balsamic vinegar in a small basin. Add pepper and salt for seasoning.

3. Pour the salad with the dressing and toss to mix.

- **Nutritional values:**
  - Calories: 350 kcal
  - Protein: 30 g
  - Carbohydrates: 20 g
  - Fat: 20 g

Chicken Tikka Masala with Cauliflower Rice

- **Preparation time (P.T.):** 35 minutes

- **Ingredients (Ingr.):**
  - 300 g chicken breast, cubed
  - 200 g Greek yogurt
  - 30 g tikka masala paste
  - 1 onion, diced (approximately 150 g)
  - 2 cloves garlic, minced (10 g)
  - 400 g diced tomatoes (canned)
  - 200 ml coconut milk
  - 300 g cauliflower, riced
  - 15 ml olive oil
  - Salt and pepper to taste

- **Servings (Serves):** 2

- **Mode of cooking:** Stovetop

- **Procedure:**

1. Put chicken, Greek yogurt, and tikka masala paste in a bowl. For a minimum of half an hour, marinate.

2. In a pan over medium heat, preheat the olive oil. Add the garlic and onion, and cook until transparent.

3. Cook the marinated chicken until it turns golden brown on all sides.

4. Stir in the coconut milk and diced tomatoes. Once the chicken is cooked through, reduce heat to a simmer and cook for 15 to 20 minutes.

5. In the interim, steam the cauliflower rice until it's soft.

6. Top cauliflower rice with chicken tikka masala.

- **Nutritional values:**
  - Calories: 400 kcal
  - Protein: 35 g
  - Carbohydrates: 20 g
  - Fat: 20 g

CHAPTER 4: CHAMPION RECOVERY: PROTEIN-PACKED MEALS TO RECHARGE YOU

Shrimp Salad with Avocado and Grapefruit

- **Preparation time (P.T.):** 15 minutes

- **Ingredients (Ingr.):**
  - 200 g cooked shrimp
  - 1 avocado, diced (approximately 150 g)
  - 1 grapefruit, segmented
  - 100 g mixed greens
  - 30 g red onion, thinly sliced
  - 30 ml olive oil
  - 15 ml lime juice
  - Salt and pepper to taste

- **Servings (Serves):** 2
- **Mode of cooking:** No cooking required
- **Procedure:**

1. In a big bowl, mix together shrimp, avocado, grapefruit segments, mixed greens, and red onion.

2. Combine lime juice and olive oil in a small bowl. Add pepper and salt for seasoning.

3. Pour the salad with the dressing and toss to mix.

- **Nutritional values:**
  - Calories: 350 kcal
  - Protein: 25 g
  - Carbohydrates: 20 g
  - Fat: 20 g

Lemon Chicken Breast with Grilled Vegetables

- **Preparation time (P.T.):** 25 minutes

- **Ingredients (Ingr.):**
  - 2 chicken breasts (approximately 300 g)
  - 30 ml olive oil
  - 1 lemon, juiced
  - 1 bell pepper, sliced (approximately 150 g)
  - 1 zucchini, sliced (approximately 200 g)
  - 1 red onion, sliced (approximately 100 g)
  - 1 tsp dried oregano (2 g)
  - Salt and pepper to taste

- **Servings (Serves):** 2

- **Mode of cooking:** Grill and stovetop

- **Procedure:**

1. Turn the heat up to medium-high on the grill.

2. In a small bowl, combine olive oil, lemon juice, oregano, salt, and pepper.

3. Coat the chicken breasts in the mixture and cook them on the grill for 7 to 8 minutes on each side, or until done.

4. Add olive oil to the cut bell pepper, zucchini, and red onion, then grill until soft.

5. Serve the grilled veggies alongside the chicken breast.

- **Nutritional values:**
    - Calories: 400 kcal
    - Protein: 35 g
    - Carbohydrates: 10 g
    - Fat: 20 g

Chocolate Mint Protein Smoothie

- **Preparation time (P.T.):** 5 minutes

- **Ingredients (Ingr.):**
    - 1 banana (approximately 120 g)
    - 30 g chocolate protein powder
    - 250 ml almond milk
    - 10 mint leaves
    - 1 tsp cocoa powder (optional)
    - 1 tsp honey (optional)

- **Servings (Serves):** 1

- **Mode of cooking:** Blender

- **Procedure:**

1. Fill a blender with all the ingredients.

2. Purée until silky.

3. Transfer into a glass and serve right away.

- **Nutritional values:**
    - Calories: 250 kcal
    - Protein: 20 g
    - Carbohydrates: 30 g
    - Fat: 5 g

Smoked Salmon with Arugula and Walnut Salad

- **Preparation time (P.T.):** 10 minutes

- **Ingredients (Ingr.):**

  - 150 g smoked salmon, sliced

  - 100 g arugula

  - 30 g walnuts, chopped

  - 1 avocado, sliced (approximately 150 g)

  - 100 g cherry tomatoes, halved

  - 30 ml olive oil

  - 15 ml lemon juice

  - Salt and pepper to taste

- **Servings (Serves):** 2

- **Mode of cooking:** No cooking required

- **Procedure:**

1. In a big bowl, mix together the arugula, walnuts, avocado, and cherry tomatoes.

2. Place slices of smoked salmon on top.

3. Combine the lemon juice and olive oil in a small bowl. Add pepper and salt for seasoning.

4. Pour the salad with the dressing and toss to mix.

- **Nutritional values:**

  - Calories: 350 kcal

  - Protein: 20 g

  - Carbohydrates: 10 g

  - Fat: 25 g

Chicken Skewers with Yogurt and Cucumber Sauce

- **Preparation time (P.T.):** 30 minutes

- **Ingredients (Ingr.):**

  - 300 g chicken breast, cut into cubes

  - 15 ml olive oil

  - 1 tsp paprika (2 g)

  - 1 tsp garlic powder (5 g)

  - 200 g Greek yogurt

  - 1 cucumber, grated (approximately 200 g)

  - 1 clove garlic, minced (5 g)

- o 15 ml lemon juice

- o Salt and pepper to taste

- **Servings (Serves):** 2

- **Mode of cooking:** Grill

- **Procedure:**

1. Turn the heat up to medium-high on the grill.

2. In a bowl, toss chicken cubes with olive oil, salt, pepper, paprika, and garlic powder.

3. After the chicken is skewered, grill it for ten to twelve minutes, turning it occasionally, until it is done.

4. In a small bowl, combine Greek yogurt, grated cucumber, chopped garlic, lemon juice, salt, and pepper.

5. Present the chicken skewers alongside cucumber sauce and yogurt.

- **Nutritional values:**

  - o Calories: 350 kcal

  - o Protein: 35 g

  - o Carbohydrates: 10 g

  - o Fat: 15 g

Tuna Salad with Green Beans and Boiled Eggs

- **Preparation time (P.T.):** 20 minutes

- **Ingredients (Ingr.):**

  - o 200 g canned tuna, drained

  - o 150 g green beans, trimmed and blanched

  - o 2 boiled eggs, sliced (approximately 100 g)

  - o 100 g cherry tomatoes, halved

  - o 30 g red onion, thinly sliced

  - o 30 ml olive oil

  - o 15 ml lemon juice

  - o Salt and pepper to taste

- **Servings (Serves):** 2

- **Mode of cooking:** No cooking required

- **Procedure:**

1. In a large bowl, mix together tuna, green beans, boiled eggs, cherry tomatoes, and red onion.

2. Combine lemon juice and olive oil in a small bowl. Add pepper and salt for seasoning.

3. Pour the salad with the dressing and toss to mix.

- **Nutritional values:**

  o Calories: 300 kcal

  o Protein: 25 g

  o Carbohydrates: 10 g

  o Fat: 20 g

Beef Steak with Cauliflower Puree

- **Preparation time (P.T.):** 30 minutes

- **Ingredients (Ingr.):**

  o 2 beef steaks (approximately 200 g each)

  o 30 ml olive oil

  o 400 g cauliflower florets

  o 50 ml heavy cream

  o 1 clove garlic, minced (5 g)

  o Salt and pepper to taste

- **Servings (Serves):** 2

- **Mode of cooking:** Grill and stovetop

- **Procedure:**

1. Turn the heat up to medium-high on the grill.

2. Season steaks with salt and pepper after brushing them with olive oil. Grill for 5 to 7 minutes on each side, or until done to taste.

3. Steam the cauliflower till it's soft in the meanwhile. Place in a blender and process until smooth, adding the heavy cream, garlic, salt, and pepper.

4. Serve pureed cauliflower alongside grilled steak.

- **Nutritional values:**

  o Calories: 450 kcal

  o Protein: 40 g

  o Carbohydrates: 10 g

  o Fat: 30 g

Vegetable Frittata with Low-Fat Cheese

- **Preparation time (P.T.):** 20 minutes

- **Ingredients (Ingr.):**

  o 6 eggs (approximately 300 g)

  o 150 g bell pepper, diced

  o 100 g spinach, chopped

- o 50 g low-fat cheese, shredded

- o 15 ml olive oil

- o Salt and pepper to taste

- **Servings (Serves):** 2

- **Mode of cooking:** Stovetop

- **Procedure:**

1. Beat the eggs in a bowl with a dash of pepper and salt.

2. In a pan over medium heat, preheat the olive oil. Cook the spinach and bell pepper together until they are tender.

3. Add the eggs to the pan and cook them until they set. Next, fold the frittata in half and sprinkle with cheese.

4. Serve right away.

- **Nutritional values:**

- o Calories: 300 kcal

- o Protein: 25 g

- o Carbohydrates: 10 g

- o Fat: 20 g

Lentil Soup with Carrots and Celery

- **Preparation time (P.T.):** 40 minutes

- **Ingredients (Ingr.):**

- o 200 g lentils, rinsed

- o 150 g carrots, diced

- o 150 g celery, diced

- o 100 g onion, diced

- o 2 cloves garlic, minced (10 g)

- o 1 liter vegetable broth

- o 15 ml olive oil

- o 1 bay leaf

- o Salt and pepper to taste

- **Servings (Serves):** 4

- **Mode of cooking:** Stovetop

- **Procedure:**

1. In a big pot over medium heat, warm the olive oil. Saute the celery, carrots, onion, and garlic until they become tender.

2. Include the bay leaf, lentils, and vegetable broth. Once the lentils are soft, bring to a boil, then lower the heat and simmer for 30 minutes.

3. Season to taste with salt and pepper. Take off the bay leaf before serving.

- **Nutritional values:**

- o Calories: 250 kcal

o   Protein: 15 g

o   Carbohydrates: 40 g

o   Fat: 5 g

Green Smoothie with Spinach, Cucumber, and Apple

- **Preparation time (P.T.):** 5 minutes

- **Ingredients (Ingr.):**

    o   100 g spinach

    o   1 cucumber, chopped (approximately 200 g)

    o   1 apple, cored and chopped (approximately 150 g)

    o   250 ml coconut water

- **Servings (Serves):** 1

- **Mode of cooking:** Blender

- **Procedure:**

1. Fill a blender with all the ingredients.

2. Purée until silky.

3. Transfer into a glass and serve right away.

- **Nutritional values:**

    o   Calories: 150 kcal

o   Protein: 5 g

o   Carbohydrates: 35 g

o   Fat: 0 g

Grilled Chicken with Mango Lime Sauce

- **Preparation time (P.T.):** 25 minutes

- **Ingredients (Ingr.):**

    o   2 chicken breasts (approximately 300 g)

    o   1 mango, peeled and diced (approximately 200 g)

    o   1 lime, juiced

    o   1 clove garlic, minced (5 g)

    o   15 ml olive oil

    o   Salt and pepper to taste

- **Servings (Serves):** 2

- **Mode of cooking:** Grill

- **Procedure:**

1. Turn the heat up to medium-high on the grill.

2. Season chicken breasts with salt and pepper after brushing them with olive oil. Cook on the grill for 7–8 minutes on each side, or until done.

3. In a blender, combine the mango, lime juice, garlic, salt, and pepper. Process till smooth.

4. Present the chicken grilled with a mango-lime sauce.

- **Nutritional values:**

  o   Calories: 350 kcal

  o   Protein: 35 g

  o   Carbohydrates: 20 g

  o   Fat: 15 g

Quinoa Salad with Shrimp and Avocado

- **Preparation time (P.T.):** 20 minutes

- **Ingredients (Ingr.):**

  o   200 g cooked shrimp

  o   150 g cooked quinoa

  o   1 avocado, diced (approximately 150 g)

  o   100 g cherry tomatoes, halved

  o   30 g red onion, thinly sliced

  o   30 ml olive oil

  o   15 ml lemon juice

  o   Salt and pepper to taste

- **Servings (Serves):** 2

- **Mode of cooking:** No cooking required

- **Procedure:**

1. In a big bowl, mix together shrimp, quinoa, avocado, cherry tomatoes, and red onion.

2. Combine lemon juice and olive oil in a small bowl. Add pepper and salt for seasoning.

3. Pour the salad with the dressing and toss to mix.

- **Nutritional values:**

  o   Calories: 350 kcal

  o   Protein: 25 g

  o   Carbohydrates: 25 g

  o   Fat: 20 g

Egg White Frittata with Spinach and Mushrooms

- **Preparation time (P.T.):** 15 minutes

- **Ingredients (Ingr.):**

  o   6 egg whites (approximately 200 g)

  o   150 g mushrooms, sliced

- o 100 g spinach, chopped

- o 15 ml olive oil

- o Salt and pepper to taste

- **Servings (Serves):** 2

- **Mode of cooking:** Stovetop

- **Procedure:**

1. In a bowl, whisk together egg whites with a dash of salt and pepper.

2. In a pan over medium heat, preheat the olive oil. Cook the spinach and mushrooms together until they are tender.

3. Add the egg whites to the pan and simmer, stirring periodically, until set.

4. Serve right away.

- **Nutritional values:**

  - o Calories: 150 kcal

  - o Protein: 20 g

  - o Carbohydrates: 5 g

  - o Fat: 5 g

Walnut-crusted cod with Asparagus

- **Preparation time (P.T.):** 25 minutes

- **Ingredients (Ingr.):**

  - o 2 cod fillets (approximately 200 g each)

  - o 50 g walnuts, chopped

  - o 1 egg, beaten (50 g)

  - o 30 ml olive oil

  - o 300 g asparagus, trimmed

  - o Salt and pepper to taste

- **Servings (Serves):** 2

- **Mode of cooking:** Oven and stovetop

- **Procedure:**

1. Set oven temperature to 190°C/375°F.

2. Coat the cod fillets with chopped walnuts after dipping them in the beaten egg.

3. In a pan over medium heat, preheat the olive oil. Brown all sides of the fish fillets.

4. Place the cod on a baking pan and cook it for ten minutes.

5. Steam asparagus for a soft texture.

6. Present steamed asparagus beside cod coated in walnuts.

- **Nutritional values:**
  - Calories: 350 kcal
  - Protein: 30 g
  - Carbohydrates: 10 g
  - Fat: 20 g

Chicken Curry with Cauliflower Rice

- **Preparation time (P.T.):** 30 minutes

- **Ingredients (Ingr.):**
  - 300 g chicken breast, cubed
  - 200 g Greek yogurt
  - 30 g curry powder
  - 1 onion, diced (approximately 150 g)
  - 2 cloves garlic, minced (10 g)
  - 400 g diced tomatoes (canned)
  - 200 ml coconut milk
  - 300 g cauliflower, riced
  - 15 ml olive oil
  - Salt and pepper to taste

- **Servings (Serves):** 2

- **Mode of cooking:** Stovetop

- **Procedure:**

1. Combine the chicken, Greek yogurt, and curry powder in a bowl. For a minimum of half an hour, marinate.

2. In a pan over medium heat, preheat the olive oil. Add the garlic and onion, and cook until transparent.

3. Cook the marinated chicken until it turns golden brown on all sides.

4. Stir in the coconut milk and diced tomatoes. Once the chicken is cooked through, reduce heat to a simmer and cook for 15 to 20 minutes.

5. In the interim, steam the cauliflower rice until it's soft.

6. Toss with cauliflower rice and serve chicken curry.

- **Nutritional values:**
  - Calories: 400 kcal
  - Protein: 35 g
  - Carbohydrates: 20 g
  - Fat: 20 g

Tuna Salad with Avocado and Cherry Tomatoes

- **Preparation time (P.T.):** 15 minutes

- **Ingredients (Ingr.):**

  o 200 g canned tuna, drained

  o 1 avocado, diced (approximately 150 g)

  o 100 g cherry tomatoes, halved

  o 30 g red onion, thinly sliced

  o 30 ml olive oil

  o 15 ml lemon juice

  o Salt and pepper to taste

- **Servings (Serves):** 2

- **Mode of cooking:** No cooking required

- **Procedure:**

1. Put the tuna, avocado, cherry tomatoes, and red onion in a big bowl.

2. Combine lemon juice and olive oil in a small bowl. Add pepper and salt for seasoning.

3. Pour the salad with the dressing and toss to mix.

- **Nutritional values:**

  o Calories: 300 kcal

  o Protein: 25 g

  o Carbohydrates: 10 g

  o Fat: 20 g

Vanilla Peanut Butter Protein Smoothie

- **Preparation time (P.T.):** 5 minutes

- **Ingredients (Ingr.):**

  o 1 banana (approximately 120 g)

  o 30 g vanilla protein powder

  o 30 g peanut butter

  o 250 ml almond milk

  o 1 tsp honey (optional)

- **Servings (Serves):** 1

- **Mode of cooking:** Blender

- **Procedure:**

1. Fill a blender with all the ingredients.

2. Purée until silky.

3. Transfer into a glass and serve right away.

- **Nutritional values:**
  - Calories: 350 kcal
  - Protein: 25 g
  - Carbohydrates: 30 g
  - Fat: 15 g

Beef Steak with Mushroom Sauce

- **Preparation time (P.T.):** 30 minutes

- **Ingredients (Ingr.):**
  - 2 beef steaks (approximately 200 g each)
  - 30 ml olive oil
  - 200 g mushrooms, sliced
  - 100 ml beef broth
  - 50 ml heavy cream
  - 1 clove garlic, minced (5 g)
  - Salt and pepper to taste

- **Servings (Serves):** 2

- **Mode of cooking:** Grill and stovetop

- **Procedure:**

1. Turn the grill's heat up to medium-high.

2. Season steaks with salt and pepper after brushing them with olive oil. Grill to desired doneness, about 5 to 7 minutes per side.

3. Heat the leftover olive oil in a pan over medium heat. Add the mushrooms and garlic, and sauté until tender.

4. Simmer the heavy cream and beef stock until the sauce thickens.

5. Top grilled steak with sauce made from mushrooms.

- **Nutritional values:**
  - Calories: 500 kcal
  - Protein: 40 g
  - Carbohydrates: 10 g
  - Fat: 35 g

Grilled Chicken with Tomato and Basil Salad

- **Preparation time (P.T.):** 20 minutes

- **Ingredients (Ingr.):**
  - 2 chicken breasts (approximately 300 g)
  - 200 g cherry tomatoes, halved

- 30 g fresh basil leaves, chopped

- 30 ml olive oil

- 15 ml balsamic vinegar

- Salt and pepper to taste

- **Servings (Serves):** 2

- **Mode of cooking:** Grill

- **Procedure:**

1. Turn the grill's heat up to medium-high.

2. Season chicken breasts with salt and pepper after brushing them with olive oil. Cook on the grill for 7–8 minutes on each side, or until well done.

3. Put the cherry tomatoes, basil, balsamic vinegar, olive oil, salt, and pepper in a bowl.

4. Accompany grilled chicken with a salad of tomatoes and basil.

- **Nutritional values:**

  - Calories: 350 kcal

  - Protein: 35 g

  - Carbohydrates: 10 g

  - Fat: 20 g

Spinach and Onion Frittata

- **Preparation time (P.T.):** 20 minutes

- **Ingredients (Ingr.):**

  - 6 eggs (approximately 300 g)

  - 150 g spinach, chopped

  - 100 g onion, diced

  - 15 ml olive oil

  - Salt and pepper to taste

- **Servings (Serves):** 2

- **Mode of cooking:** Stovetop

- **Procedure:**

1. Beat the eggs in a bowl with a dash of pepper and salt.

2. In a pan over medium heat, preheat the olive oil. Cook the spinach and onion until they are tender.

3. Add the eggs to the pan and cook them until they set. Serve the frittata right away after folding it in half.

- **Nutritional values:**

  - Calories: 250 kcal

  - Protein: 20 g

  - Carbohydrates: 5 g

  - Fat: 18 g

CHAPTER 5: TOP MUSCLE: NUTRITIOUS DELIGHTS TO REJUVENATE YOU

Roasted Chicken with Sweet Potatoes

- **Preparation time (P.T.):** 40 minutes

- **Ingredients (Ingr.):**

    o 2 chicken thighs (approximately 300 g)

    o 400 g sweet potatoes, diced

    o 30 ml olive oil

    o 1 tsp garlic powder (5 g)

    o 1 tsp paprika (5 g)

    o Salt and pepper to taste

- **Servings (Serves):** 2

- **Mode of cooking:** Oven

- **Procedure:**

1. Set oven temperature to 200°C/400°F.

2. Combine sweet potatoes, olive oil, paprika, garlic powder, salt, and pepper in a baking dish.

3. Top the sweet potatoes with the chicken thighs, then sprinkle with salt and pepper.

4. Bake for 35 to 40 minutes, or until the sweet potatoes are soft and the chicken is thoroughly cooked.

5. Present right away.

- **Nutritional values:**

    o Calories: 500 kcal

    o Protein: 30 g

    o Carbohydrates: 45 g

    o Fat: 20 g

Quinoa Salad with Feta and Cherry Tomatoes

- **Preparation time (P.T.):** 15 minutes

- **Ingredients (Ingr.):**

    o 150 g cooked quinoa

    o 100 g cherry tomatoes, halved

    o 50 g feta cheese, crumbled

    o 30 g red onion, thinly sliced

    o 30 ml olive oil

    o 15 ml lemon juice

    o Salt and pepper to taste

- **Servings (Serves):** 2

- **Mode of cooking:** No cooking required

- **Procedure:**

1. Combine the quinoa, red onion, feta cheese, and cherry tomatoes in a big bowl.

2. Combine lemon juice and olive oil in a small bowl. Add pepper and salt for seasoning.

3. Pour the salad with the dressing and toss to mix.

- **Nutritional values:**

  - Calories: 350 kcal

  - Protein: 15 g

  - Carbohydrates: 35 g

  - Fat: 20 g

Lentil Meatballs with Tomato Sauce

- **Preparation time (P.T.):** 45 minutes

- **Ingredients (Ingr.):**

  - 200 g lentils, cooked and mashed

  - 50 g breadcrumbs

  - 1 egg (50 g)

  - 2 cloves garlic, minced (10 g)

  - 1 tsp dried oregano (2 g)

  - 400 g tomato sauce

  - 30 ml olive oil

  - Salt and pepper to taste

- **Servings (Serves):** 4

- **Mode of cooking:** Oven and stovetop

- **Procedure:**

1. Set oven temperature to 190°C/375°F.

2. Put the egg, breadcrumbs, garlic, oregano, salt, and pepper in a bowl along with the mashed lentils. Shape into meatballs.

3. In a pan over medium heat, preheat the olive oil. Burgers should be browned all over.

4. Move the meatballs to a baking tray and cover them with tomato sauce.

5. Bake for 25 to 30 minutes in the oven.

6. Serve tomato sauce with meatballs.

- **Nutritional values:**

  - Calories: 300 kcal

  - Protein: 15 g

  - Carbohydrates: 40 g

  - Fat: 10 g

Grilled Fish with Cucumber Salad

- **Preparation time (P.T.):** 20 minutes

- **Ingredients (Ingr.):**

  - 2 white fish fillets (approximately 200 g each)

  - 15 ml olive oil

  - 1 cucumber, thinly sliced (approximately 200 g)

  - 100 g cherry tomatoes, halved

  - 30 g red onion, thinly sliced

  - 30 ml olive oil

  - 15 ml lemon juice

  - Salt and pepper to taste

- **Servings (Serves):** 2

- **Mode of cooking:** Grill and no cooking required

- **Procedure:**

1. Turn the grill's heat up to medium-high.

2. Season fish fillets with salt and pepper after brushing them with olive oil. Cook on the grill for 4–5 minutes on each side, or until done.

3. Combine cucumber, cherry tomatoes, and red onion in a big bowl.

4. Combine the lemon juice and olive oil in a small bowl. Add pepper and salt for seasoning.

5. Pour the salad with the dressing and toss to mix.

6. Serve cucumber salad beside grilled fish.

- **Nutritional values:**

  - Calories: 300 kcal

  - Protein: 30 g

  - Carbohydrates: 10 g

  - Fat: 15 g

Eggs Benedict with Spinach

- **Preparation time (P.T.):** 25 minutes

- **Ingredients (Ingr.):**

  - 2 English muffins, split (approximately 100 g)

  - 4 eggs (approximately 200 g)

  - 200 g spinach, washed and chopped

  - 100 g smoked salmon, sliced

- o 100 ml hollandaise sauce

- o 15 ml olive oil

- o Salt and pepper to taste

- **Servings (Serves):** 2

- **Mode of cooking:** Stovetop

- **Procedure:**

1. Preheat the muffin tin.

2. In a pan over medium heat, preheat the olive oil. When the spinach begins to wilt, add it.

3. Simmer the eggs in the water until the whites are set, about 3 to 4 minutes.

4. Arrange spinach, poached egg, smoked salmon, and hollandaise sauce on top of each muffin half.

5. Season to taste with salt and pepper, then serve right away.

- **Nutritional values:**

- o Calories: 450 kcal

- o Protein: 25 g

- o Carbohydrates: 30 g

- o Fat: 25 g

Chicken Salad with Almonds and Grapes

- **Preparation time (P.T.):** 15 minutes

- **Ingredients (Ingr.):**

- o 200 g cooked chicken breast, diced

- o 50 g almonds, sliced

- o 150 g grapes, halved

- o 100 g celery, diced

- o 50 g Greek yogurt

- o 15 ml lemon juice

- o Salt and pepper to taste

- **Servings (Serves):** 2

- **Mode of cooking:** No cooking required

- **Procedure:**

1. Combine the chicken, celery, grapes, and almonds in a big bowl.

2. Combine Greek yogurt, lemon juice, salt, and pepper in a small bowl.

3. Include the salad in the dressing and toss to mix.

4. Serve right away.

- **Nutritional values:**
  - Calories: 300 kcal
  - Protein: 25 g
  - Carbohydrates: 20 g
  - Fat: 15 g

Mixed Berry Protein Smoothie

- **Preparation time (P.T.):** 5 minutes
- **Ingredients (Ingr.):**
  - 100 g mixed berries (strawberries, blueberries, raspberries)
  - 30 g vanilla protein powder
  - 250 ml almond milk
  - 1 tsp honey (optional)
- **Servings (Serves):** 1
- **Mode of cooking:** Blender
- **Procedure:**

1. Fill a blender with all the ingredients.

2. Purée until silky.

3. Transfer into a glass and serve right away.

- **Nutritional values:**
  - Calories: 200 kcal
  - Protein: 20 g
  - Carbohydrates: 25 g
  - Fat: 5 g

Oven-Roasted Turkey with Steamed Vegetables

- **Preparation time (P.T.):** 45 minutes
- **Ingredients (Ingr.):**
  - 400 g turkey breast, sliced
  - 30 ml olive oil
  - 1 tsp dried thyme (2 g)
  - 1 tsp garlic powder (5 g)
  - 200 g broccoli florets
  - 200 g carrots, sliced
  - Salt and pepper to taste
- **Servings (Serves):** 2
- **Mode of cooking:** Oven and stovetop
- **Procedure:**

1. Set oven temperature to 190°C/375°F.

2. Apply salt, pepper, garlic powder, thyme, and olive oil to the turkey breast.

3. Bake for 35 to 40 minutes, or until thoroughly done, for roasting.

4. In the interim, simmer carrots and broccoli until they are soft.

5. Present the cooked turkey alongside steaming veggies.

- **Nutritional values:**

  - Calories: 350 kcal

  - Protein: 30 g

  - Carbohydrates: 15 g

  - Fat: 15 g

Kale Salad with Avocado and Pumpkin Seeds

- **Preparation time (P.T.):** 10 minutes

- **Ingredients (Ingr.):**

  - 150 g kale, chopped

  - 1 avocado, diced (approximately 150 g)

  - 30 g pumpkin seeds

  - 100 g cherry tomatoes, halved

  - 30 ml olive oil

  - 15 ml lemon juice

  - Salt and pepper to taste

- **Servings (Serves):** 2

- **Mode of cooking:** No cooking required

- **Procedure:**

1. Combine the kale, avocado, pumpkin seeds, and cherry tomatoes in a big bowl.

2. Combine lemon juice and olive oil in a small bowl. Add pepper and salt for seasoning.

3. Pour the salad with the dressing and toss to mix.

4. Serve right away.

- **Nutritional values:**

  - Calories: 300 kcal

  - Protein: 10 g

  - Carbohydrates: 20 g

  - Fat: 20 g

Egg White Frittata with Peppers and Onions

- **Preparation time (P.T.):** 15 minutes

- **Ingredients (Ingr.):**

  - 6 egg whites (approximately 200 g)

  - 150 g bell pepper, diced

  - 100 g onion, diced

  - 15 ml olive oil

  - Salt and pepper to taste

- **Servings (Serves):** 2

- **Mode of cooking:** Stovetop

- **Procedure:**

1. Beat egg whites in a bowl with a dash of pepper and salt.

2. In a pan over medium heat, preheat the olive oil. Add onion and bell pepper, and sauté until tender.

3. Add the egg whites to the pan and simmer, stirring periodically, until set.

4. Serve right away.

- **Nutritional values:**

  - Calories: 150 kcal

  - Protein: 20 g

  - Carbohydrates: 5 g

  - Fat: 5 g

Chicken Curry with Basmati Rice

- **Preparation time (P.T.):** 35 minutes

- **Ingredients (Ingr.):**

  - 300 g chicken breast, cubed

  - 200 g Greek yogurt

  - 30 g curry powder

  - 1 onion, diced (approximately 150 g)

  - 2 cloves garlic, minced (10 g)

  - 400 g diced tomatoes (canned)

  - 200 ml coconut milk

  - 180 g basmati rice

  - 15 ml olive oil

  - Salt and pepper to taste

- **Servings (Serves):** 2

- **Mode of cooking:** Stovetop

- **Procedure:**

1. Combine the chicken, Greek yogurt, and curry powder in a bowl. For a minimum of half an hour, marinate.

2. Prepare basmati rice as directed on the package.

3. In a pan over medium heat, preheat the olive oil. Add the garlic and onion, and cook until transparent.

4. Cook the marinated chicken until it turns golden brown on all sides.

5. Stir in the coconut milk and diced tomatoes. Once the chicken is cooked through, reduce heat to a simmer and cook for 15 to 20 minutes.

6. Spoon curry chicken over basmati rice.

- **Nutritional values:**

    o   Calories: 500 kcal

    o   Protein: 35 g

    o   Carbohydrates: 50 g

    o   Fat: 20 g

Tuna Salad with Black Beans and Corn

- **Preparation time (P.T.):** 15 minutes

- **Ingredients (Ingr.):**

    o   200 g canned tuna, drained

    o   150 g black beans, rinsed and drained

    o   150 g corn kernels

    o   100 g cherry tomatoes, halved

    o   30 g red onion, thinly sliced

    o   30 ml olive oil

    o   15 ml lime juice

    o   Salt and pepper to taste

- **Servings (Serves):** 2

- **Mode of cooking:** No cooking required

- **Procedure:**

1. Combine the tuna, red onion, cherry tomatoes, black beans, and corn in a big bowl.

2. Combine lime juice and olive oil in a small bowl. Add pepper and salt for seasoning.

3. Pour the salad with the dressing and toss to mix.

4. Serve right away.

- **Nutritional values:**

    o   Calories: 350 kcal

    o   Protein: 25 g

    o   Carbohydrates: 30 g

    o   Fat: 15 g

Grilled Chicken with Yogurt and Cucumber Sauce

- **Preparation time (P.T.):** 25 minutes

- **Ingredients (Ingr.):**

  - 2 chicken breasts (approximately 300 g)

  - 30 ml olive oil

  - 200 g Greek yogurt

  - 1 cucumber, grated (approximately 200 g)

  - 1 clove garlic, minced (5 g)

  - 15 ml lemon juice

  - 1 tsp dried dill (2 g)

  - Salt and pepper to taste

- **Servings (Serves):** 2

- **Mode of cooking:** Grill and no cooking required

- **Procedure:**

1. Turn the grill's heat up to medium-high.

2. Season chicken breasts with salt and pepper after brushing them with olive oil. Cook on the grill for 7–8 minutes on each side, or until well done.

3. Combine Greek yogurt, grated cucumber, dill, lemon juice, garlic, and salt and pepper in a small bowl.

4. Present the grilled chicken together with cucumber sauce and yogurt.

- **Nutritional values:**

  - Calories: 300 kcal

  - Protein: 35 g

  - Carbohydrates: 10 g

  - Fat: 15 g

Spinach and Sun-Dried Tomato Frittata

- **Preparation time (P.T.):** 20 minutes

- **Ingredients (Ingr.):**

  - 6 eggs (approximately 300 g)

  - 150 g spinach, chopped

  - 50 g sun-dried tomatoes, chopped

  - 50 g low-fat cheese, shredded

  - 15 ml olive oil

  - Salt and pepper to taste

- **Servings (Serves):** 2

- **Mode of cooking:** Stovetop

- **Procedure:**

1. Beat the eggs in a bowl with a dash of pepper and salt.

2. In a pan over medium heat, preheat the olive oil. Cook the spinach until it softens, then add the sun-dried tomatoes.

3. Add the eggs to the pan and cook them until they set. Next, fold the frittata in half and sprinkle with cheese.

4. Serve right away.

- **Nutritional values:**

  - Calories: 300 kcal

  - Protein: 25 g

  - Carbohydrates: 10 g

  - Fat: 20 g

Shrimp Salad with Avocado and Lime

- **Preparation time (P.T.):** 15 minutes

- **Ingredients (Ingr.):**

  - 200 g cooked shrimp

  - 1 avocado, diced (approximately 150 g)

  - 100 g cherry tomatoes, halved

  - 30 g red onion, thinly sliced

  - 30 ml olive oil

  - 15 ml lime juice

  - Salt and pepper to taste

- **Servings (Serves):** 2

- **Mode of cooking:** No cooking required

- **Procedure:**

1. Put the shrimp, avocado, cherry tomatoes, and red onion in a big bowl.

2. Combine lime juice and olive oil in a small bowl. Add pepper and salt for seasoning.

3. Pour the salad with the dressing and toss to mix.

4. Serve right away.

- **Nutritional values:**

  - Calories: 350 kcal

  - Protein: 25 g

  - Carbohydrates: 15 g

  - Fat: 20 g

Chocolate Mint Protein Smoothie

- **Preparation time (P.T.):** 5 minutes

- **Ingredients (Ingr.):**

  - 1 banana (approximately 120 g)

  - 30 g chocolate protein powder

  - 250 ml almond milk

  - 10 mint leaves

  - 1 tsp cocoa powder (optional)

  - 1 tsp honey (optional)

- **Servings (Serves):** 1

- **Mode of cooking:** Blender

- **Procedure:**

1. Fill a blender with all the ingredients.

2. Purée until silky.

3. Transfer into a glass and serve right away.

- **Nutritional values:**

  - Calories: 250 kcal

  - Protein: 20 g

  - Carbohydrates: 30 g

  - Fat: 5 g

Almond-Crusted Cod with Broccoli

- **Preparation time (P.T.):** 25 minutes

- **Ingredients (Ingr.):**

  - 2 cod fillets (approximately 200 g each)

  - 50 g ground almonds

  - 1 egg, beaten (50 g)

  - 30 ml olive oil

  - 300 g broccoli florets

  - Salt and pepper to taste

- **Servings (Serves):** 2

- **Mode of cooking:** Oven and stovetop

- **Procedure:**

1. Set oven temperature to 190°C/375°F.

2. Coat the fish fillets with ground almonds after dipping them in the beaten egg.

3. In a pan over medium heat, preheat the olive oil. Brown all sides of the fish fillets.

4. After moving the cod to a baking sheet, bake it for ten minutes, or until it is well done.

5. Cook broccoli in steam until soft.

6. Present cod coated in almonds alongside steaming broccoli.

- **Nutritional values:**

    o Calories: 350 kcal

    o Protein: 30 g

    o Carbohydrates: 10 g

    o Fat: 20 g

Paprika Chicken with Sweet Potatoes

- **Preparation time (P.T.):** 40 minutes

- **Ingredients (Ingr.):**

    o 2 chicken thighs (approximately 300 g)

    o 400 g sweet potatoes, diced

    o 30 ml olive oil

    o 1 tsp paprika (5 g)

    o 1 tsp garlic powder (5 g)

    o Salt and pepper to taste

- **Servings (Serves):** 2

- **Mode of cooking:** Oven

- **Procedure:**

1. Set oven temperature to 200°C/400°F.

2. Combine sweet potatoes, olive oil, paprika, garlic powder, salt, and pepper in a baking dish.

3. Top the sweet potatoes with the chicken thighs, then sprinkle with salt and pepper.

4. Bake for 35 to 40 minutes, or until the sweet potatoes are soft and the chicken is thoroughly cooked.

5. Present right away.

- **Nutritional values:**

    o Calories: 500 kcal

    o Protein: 30 g

    o Carbohydrates: 45 g

    o Fat: 20 g

Egg White Frittata with Zucchini and Onions

- **Preparation time (P.T.):** 15 minutes

- **Ingredients (Ingr.):**

    o 6 egg whites (approximately 200 g)

- o 150 g zucchini, diced

- o 100 g onion, diced

- o 15 ml olive oil

- o Salt and pepper to taste

- **Servings (Serves):** 2

- **Mode of cooking:** Stovetop

- **Procedure:**

1. Beat egg whites in a bowl with a dash of pepper and salt.

2. In a pan over medium heat, preheat the olive oil. Cook the onion and zucchini until they are tender.

3. Add the egg whites to the pan and simmer, stirring periodically, until set.

4. Serve right away.

- **Nutritional values:**

  - o Calories: 150 kcal

  - o Protein: 20 g

  - o Carbohydrates: 5 g

  - o Fat: 5 g

Tuna Salad with Green Beans and Olives

- **Preparation time (P.T.):** 15 minutes

- **Ingredients (Ingr.):**

  - o 200 g canned tuna, drained

  - o 150 g green beans, trimmed and blanched

  - o 50 g black olives, sliced

  - o 100 g cherry tomatoes, halved

  - o 30 g red onion, thinly sliced

  - o 30 ml olive oil

  - o 15 ml lemon juice

  - o Salt and pepper to taste

- **Servings (Serves):** 2

- **Mode of cooking:** No cooking required

- **Procedure:**

1. Put the tuna, green beans, cherry tomatoes, olives, and red onion in a big bowl.

2. Combine lemon juice and olive oil in a small bowl. Add pepper and salt for seasoning.

3. Pour the salad with the dressing and toss to mix.

4. Serve right away.

- **Nutritional values:**
  - Calories: 300 kcal
  - Protein: 25 g
  - Carbohydrates: 10 g
  - Fat: 20 g

Grilled Chicken with Lemon Herb Sauce

- **Preparation time (P.T.):** 20 minutes
- **Ingredients (Ingr.):**
  - 2 chicken breasts (approximately 300 g)
  - 30 ml olive oil
  - 1 lemon, juiced
  - 1 tsp dried thyme (2 g)
  - 1 tsp dried rosemary (2 g)
  - Salt and pepper to taste
- **Servings (Serves):** 2
- **Mode of cooking:** Grill

- **Procedure:**

1. Turn the grill's heat up to medium-high.

2. Combine the olive oil, lemon juice, rosemary, thyme, salt, and pepper in a small bowl.

3. Grill the chicken breasts for 7 to 8 minutes on each side, or until they are cooked through, after brushing them with the mixture.

4. Serve right away.

- **Nutritional values:**
  - Calories: 300 kcal
  - Protein: 35 g
  - Carbohydrates: 5 g
  - Fat: 15 g

Spinach and Mushroom Frittata

- **Preparation time (P.T.):** 20 minutes
- **Ingredients (Ingr.):**
  - 6 eggs (approximately 300 g)
  - 150 g spinach, chopped
  - 150 g mushrooms, sliced
  - 15 ml olive oil

- o Salt and pepper to taste
- **Servings (Serves):** 2
- **Mode of cooking:** Stovetop
- **Procedure:**

1. Beat the eggs in a bowl with a dash of pepper and salt.

2. In a pan over medium heat, preheat the olive oil. Cook the spinach and mushrooms until they become tender.

3. Add the eggs to the pan and cook them until they set. Serve the frittata right away after folding it in half.

- **Nutritional values:**
    - o Calories: 250 kcal
    - o Protein: 20 g
    - o Carbohydrates: 5 g
    - o Fat: 18 g

Grilled Salmon with Asparagus and Quinoa

- **Preparation time (P.T.):** 25 minutes
- **Ingredients (Ingr.):**
    - o 2 salmon fillets (approximately 200 g each)
    - o 450 g asparagus, trimmed
    - o 180 g quinoa
    - o 500 ml vegetable broth
    - o 30 ml olive oil
    - o Salt and pepper to taste
- **Servings (Serves):** 2
- **Mode of cooking:** Grill and stovetop
- **Procedure:**

1. Turn the grill's heat up to medium-high.

2. Season salmon fillets with salt and pepper after brushing them with olive oil. Cook on the grill for 7–8 minutes on each side, or until well done.

3. Prepare the quinoa in the veggie broth per the directions on the package.

4. Steam asparagus for a soft texture.

5. Present asparagus and quinoa beside grilled fish.

- **Nutritional values:**
    - o Calories: 500 kcal
    - o Protein: 40 g
    - o Carbohydrates: 30 g
    - o Fat: 20 g

Chicken Curry with Brown Rice

- **Preparation time (P.T.):** 35 minutes

- **Ingredients (Ingr.):**

    - 300 g chicken breast, cubed

    - 200 g Greek yogurt

    - 30 g curry powder

    - 1 onion, diced (approximately 150 g)

    - 2 cloves garlic, minced (10 g)

    - 400 g diced tomatoes (canned)

    - 200 ml coconut milk

    - 180 g brown rice

    - 15 ml olive oil

    - Salt and pepper to taste

- **Servings (Serves):** 2

- **Mode of cooking:** Stovetop

- **Procedure:**

1. Combine the chicken, Greek yogurt, and curry powder in a bowl. For a minimum of half an hour, marinate.

2. Prepare brown rice as directed on the package.

3. In a pan over medium heat, preheat the olive oil. Add the garlic and onion, and cook until transparent.

4. Cook the marinated chicken until it turns golden brown on all sides.

5. Stir in the coconut milk and diced tomatoes. Once the chicken is cooked through, reduce heat to a simmer and cook for 15 to 20 minutes.

6. Spoon brown rice over chicken curry.

- **Nutritional values:**

    - Calories: 500 kcal

    - Protein: 35 g

    - Carbohydrates: 50 g

    - Fat: 20 g

Chicken Salad with Avocado and Walnuts

- **Preparation time (P.T.):** 15 minutes

- **Ingredients (Ingr.):**

    - 200 g cooked chicken breast, diced

    - 1 avocado, diced (approximately 150 g)

    - 50 g walnuts, chopped

    - 100 g cherry tomatoes, halved

- o 30 g red onion, thinly sliced

- o 30 ml olive oil

- o 15 ml lemon juice

- o Salt and pepper to taste

- **Servings (Serves):** 2

- **Mode of cooking:** No cooking required

- **Procedure:**

1. Put the chicken, avocado, walnuts, cherry tomatoes, and red onion in a big bowl.

2. Combine lemon juice and olive oil in a small bowl. Add pepper and salt for seasoning.

3. Pour the salad with the dressing and toss to mix.

4. Serve right away.

- **Nutritional values:**

  - o Calories: 400 kcal

  - o Protein: 30 g

  - o Carbohydrates: 15 g

  - o Fat: 25 g

Chocolate Banana Protein Smoothie

- **Preparation time (P.T.):** 5 minutes

- **Ingredients (Ingr.):**

  - o 1 banana (approximately 120 g)

  - o 30 g chocolate protein powder

  - o 250 ml almond milk

  - o 1 tsp cocoa powder (optional)

  - o 1 tsp honey (optional)

- **Servings (Serves):** 1

- **Mode of cooking:** Blender

- **Procedure:**

1. Fill a blender with all the ingredients.

2. Purée until silky.

3. Transfer into a glass and serve right away.

- **Nutritional values:**

  - o Calories: 250 kcal

  - o Protein: 20 g

  - o Carbohydrates: 30 g

  - o Fat: 5 g

Baked Cod with Sweet Potatoes and Spinach

- **Preparation time (P.T.):** 30 minutes

- **Ingredients (Ingr.):**

    o 2 cod fillets (approximately 200 g each)

    o 400 g sweet potatoes, diced

    o 200 g spinach, washed and chopped

    o 30 ml olive oil

    o 1 tsp garlic powder (5 g)

    o Salt and pepper to taste

- **Servings (Serves):** 2

- **Mode of cooking:** Oven and stovetop

- **Procedure:**

1. Set oven temperature to 190°C/375°F.

2. Combine salt, pepper, garlic powder, and olive oil with sweet potatoes. Place on a baking pan, then bake until soft, about 25 minutes.

3. In the interim, sprinkle salt and pepper on the fish fillets. Transfer to a baking sheet and heat for 10 to 12 minutes, or until well done.

4. Cook spinach in steam until it wilts.

5. Present cooked cod alongside spinach and sweet potatoes.

- **Nutritional values:**

    o Calories: 350 kcal

    o Protein: 30 g

    o Carbohydrates: 40 g

    o Fat: 10 g

Turmeric Chicken with Steamed Vegetables

- **Preparation time (P.T.):** 30 minutes

- **Ingredients (Ingr.):**

    o 2 chicken breasts (approximately 300 g)

    o 1 tsp turmeric (5 g)

    o 1 tsp garlic powder (5 g)

    o 30 ml olive oil

    o 200 g broccoli florets

    o 200 g carrots, sliced

    o Salt and pepper to taste

- **Servings (Serves):** 2
- **Mode of cooking:** Stovetop and steaming
- **Procedure:**

1. Combine the garlic powder, salt, pepper, and turmeric in a bowl. Coat the chicken breasts with the mixture.

2. In a pan over medium heat, preheat the olive oil. Cook chicken breasts until cooked through, about 7 to 8 minutes per side.

3. Steam carrots and broccoli until they are soft.

4. Accompany the chicken with turmeric by steaming veggies.

- **Nutritional values:**
    - Calories: 350 kcal
    - Protein: 35 g
    - Carbohydrates: 15 g
    - Fat: 15 g

Red Pepper and Onion Frittata

- **Preparation time (P.T.):** 20 minutes
- **Ingredients (Ingr.):**
    - 6 eggs (approximately 300 g)
    - 150 g red bell pepper, diced
    - 100 g onion, diced
    - 15 ml olive oil
    - Salt and pepper to taste
- **Servings (Serves):** 2
- **Mode of cooking:** Stovetop
- **Procedure:**

1. Beat the eggs in a bowl with a dash of pepper and salt.

2. In a pan over medium heat, preheat the olive oil. When the onion and red bell pepper are soft, add them and simmer.

3. Add the eggs to the pan and cook them until they set. Serve the frittata right away after folding it in half.

- **Nutritional values:**
    - Calories: 250 kcal
    - Protein: 20 g
    - Carbohydrates: 5 g
    - Fat: 18 g

Tuna Salad with Chickpeas and Peppers

- **Preparation time (P.T.):** 15 minutes

- **Ingredients (Ingr.):**

  - 200 g canned tuna, drained

  - 150 g chickpeas, rinsed and drained

  - 150 g bell pepper, diced

  - 100 g cherry tomatoes, halved

  - 30 g red onion, thinly sliced

  - 30 ml olive oil

  - 15 ml lemon juice

  - Salt and pepper to taste

- **Servings (Serves):** 2

- **Mode of cooking:** No cooking required

- **Procedure:**

1. Put the bell pepper, cherry tomatoes, red onion, chickpeas, and tuna in a big bowl.

2. Combine lemon juice and olive oil in a small bowl. Add pepper and salt for seasoning.

3. Pour the salad with the dressing and toss to mix.

4. Serve right away.

- **Nutritional values:**

  - Calories: 300 kcal

  - Protein: 25 g

  - Carbohydrates: 20 g

  - Fat: 15 g

Grilled Chicken with Avocado Sauce

- **Preparation time (P.T.):** 20 minutes

- **Ingredients (Ingr.):**

  - 2 chicken breasts (approximately 300 g)

  - 1 avocado, mashed (approximately 150 g)

  - 30 ml Greek yogurt

  - 15 ml lime juice

  - 1 clove garlic, minced (5 g)

  - 30 ml olive oil

  - Salt and pepper to taste

- **Servings (Serves):** 2

- **Mode of cooking:** Grill and no cooking required

- **Procedure:**

1. Turn the grill's heat up to medium-high.

2. Season chicken breasts with salt and pepper after brushing them with olive oil. Cook on the grill for 7–8 minutes on each side, or until well done.

3. Combine Greek yogurt, mashed avocado, lime juice, garlic, salt, and pepper in a small bowl.

4. Present avocado sauce beside grilled chicken.

- **Nutritional values:**

    o Calories: 350 kcal

    o Protein: 35 g

    o Carbohydrates: 10 g

    o Fat: 20 g

Egg White Frittata with Spinach and Green Onions

- **Preparation time (P.T.):** 15 minutes

- **Ingredients (Ingr.):**

    o 6 egg whites (approximately 200 g)

    o 100 g spinach, chopped

    o 50 g green onions, sliced

    o 15 ml olive oil

    o Salt and pepper to taste

- **Servings (Serves):** 2

- **Mode of cooking:** Stovetop

- **Procedure:**

1. Beat egg whites in a bowl with a dash of pepper and salt.

2. In a pan over medium heat, preheat the olive oil. When the spinach and green onions are soft, add them and simmer.

3. Add the egg whites to the pan and simmer, stirring periodically, until set.

4. Serve right away.

- **Nutritional values:**

    o Calories: 150 kcal

    o Protein: 20 g

    o Carbohydrates: 5 g

    o Fat: 5 g

Shrimp Salad with Avocado and Grapefruit

- **Preparation time (P.T.):** 15 minutes

- **Ingredients (Ingr.):**

  - 200 g cooked shrimp

  - 1 avocado, diced (approximately 150 g)

  - 1 grapefruit, segmented

  - 100 g mixed greens

  - 30 g red onion, thinly sliced

  - 30 ml olive oil

  - 15 ml lime juice

  - Salt and pepper to taste

- **Servings (Serves):** 2

- **Mode of cooking:** No cooking required

- **Procedure:**

1. Put the shrimp, avocado, grapefruit segments, mixed greens, and red onion in a big bowl.

2. Combine lime juice and olive oil in a small bowl. Add pepper and salt for seasoning.

3. Pour the salad with the dressing and toss to mix.

4. Serve right away.

- **Nutritional values:**

  - Calories: 350 kcal

  - Protein: 25 g

  - Carbohydrates: 20 g

  - Fat: 20 g

Lemon Chicken Breast with Grilled Vegetables

- **Preparation time (P.T.):** 25 minutes

- **Ingredients (Ingr.):**

  - 2 chicken breasts (approximately 300 g)

  - 30 ml olive oil

  - 1 lemon, juiced

  - 1 bell pepper, sliced (approximately 150 g)

  - 1 zucchini, sliced (approximately 200 g)

  - 1 red onion, sliced (approximately 100 g)

  - 1 tsp dried oregano (2 g)

  - Salt and pepper to taste

- **Servings (Serves):** 2

- **Mode of cooking:** Grill and stovetop

- **Procedure:**

1. Turn the grill's heat up to medium-high.

2. Combine the olive oil, lemon juice, oregano, salt, and pepper in a small bowl.

3. Grill the chicken breasts for 7 to 8 minutes on each side, or until they are cooked through, after brushing them with the mixture.

4. Toss the red onion, zucchini, and bell pepper slices with the leftover olive oil and grill until soft.

5. Serve the grilled veggies alongside the chicken breast.

- **Nutritional values:**
  - Calories: 400 kcal
  - Protein: 35 g
  - Carbohydrates: 10 g
  - Fat: 20 g

Chocolate Mint Protein Smoothie

- **Preparation time (P.T.):** 5 minutes

- **Ingredients (Ingr.):**
  - 1 banana (approximately 120 g)
  - 30 g chocolate protein powder
  - 250 ml almond milk
  - 10 mint leaves
  - 1 tsp cocoa powder (optional)
  - 1 tsp honey (optional)

- **Servings (Serves):** 1
- **Mode of cooking:** Blender
- **Procedure:**

1. Fill a blender with all the ingredients.

2. Purée until silky.

3. Transfer into a glass and serve right away.

- **Nutritional values:**
  - Calories: 250 kcal
  - Protein: 20 g
  - Carbohydrates: 30 g
  - Fat: 5 g

Smoked Salmon with Arugula and Walnut Salad

- **Preparation time (P.T.):** 10 minutes

- **Ingredients (Ingr.):**

  - 150 g smoked salmon, sliced

  - 100 g arugula

  - 30 g walnuts, chopped

  - 1 avocado, sliced (approximately 150 g)

  - 100 g cherry tomatoes, halved

  - 30 ml olive oil

  - 15 ml lemon juice

  - Salt and pepper to taste

- **Servings (Serves):** 2

- **Mode of cooking:** No cooking required

- **Procedure:**

1. Combine the avocado, cherry tomatoes, walnuts, and arugula in a big bowl.

2. Place slices of smoked salmon on top.

3. Combine the lemon juice and olive oil in a small bowl. Add pepper and salt for seasoning.

4. Pour the salad with the dressing and toss to mix.

5. Present right away.

- **Nutritional values:**

  - Calories: 350 kcal

  - Protein: 20 g

  - Carbohydrates: 10 g

  - Fat: 25 g

Chicken Skewers with Yogurt and Cucumber Sauce

- **Preparation time (P.T.):** 30 minutes

- **Ingredients (Ingr.):**

  - 300 g chicken breast, cut into cubes

  - 15 ml olive oil

  - 1 tsp paprika (2 g)

  - 1 tsp garlic powder (5 g)

  - 200 g Greek yogurt

  - 1 cucumber, grated (approximately 200 g)

- o 1 clove garlic, minced (5 g)

- o 15 ml lemon juice

- o Salt and pepper to taste

- **Servings (Serves):** 2

- **Mode of cooking:** Grill

- **Procedure:**

1. Turn the grill's heat up to medium-high.

2. Combine the olive oil, paprika, garlic powder, salt, and pepper in a bowl with the chicken chunks.

3. After the chicken is threaded onto skewers, grill it for ten to twelve minutes, turning it occasionally, until it is thoroughly cooked.

4. Combine Greek yogurt, minced garlic, grated cucumber, lemon juice, salt, and pepper in a small bowl.

5. Present the chicken skewers alongside cucumber sauce and yogurt.

- **Nutritional values:**

- o Calories: 350 kcal

- o Protein: 35 g

- o Carbohydrates: 10 g

- o Fat: 15 g

Tuna Salad with Green Beans and Boiled Eggs

- **Preparation time (P.T.):** 20 minutes

- **Ingredients (Ingr.):**

- o 200 g canned tuna, drained

- o 150 g green beans, trimmed and blanched

- o 2 boiled eggs, sliced (approximately 100 g)

- o 100 g cherry tomatoes, halved

- o 30 g red onion, thinly sliced

- o 30 ml olive oil

- o 15 ml lemon juice

- o Salt and pepper to taste

- **Servings (Serves):** 2

- **Mode of cooking:** No cooking required

- **Procedure:**

1. Put the tuna, red onion, cherry tomatoes, green beans, and boiled eggs in a big bowl.

2. Combine lemon juice and olive oil in a small bowl. Add pepper and salt for seasoning.

3. Pour the salad with the dressing and toss to mix.

4. Serve right away.

- **Nutritional values:**
    - Calories: 300 kcal
    - Protein: 25 g
    - Carbohydrates: 10 g
    - Fat: 20 g

Beef Steak with Cauliflower Puree

- **Preparation time (P.T.):** 30 minutes
- **Ingredients (Ingr.):**
    - 2 beef steaks (approximately 200 g each)
    - 30 ml olive oil
    - 400 g cauliflower florets
    - 50 ml heavy cream
    - 1 clove garlic, minced (5 g)
    - Salt and pepper to taste
- **Servings (Serves):** 2

- **Mode of cooking:** Grill and stovetop
- **Procedure:**

1. Turn the grill's heat up to medium-high.

2. Season steaks with salt and pepper after brushing them with olive oil. Grill to desired doneness, about 5 to 7 minutes per side.

3. Steam the cauliflower till it's soft in the meanwhile. Place in a blender and process until smooth, adding the heavy cream, garlic, salt, and pepper.

4. Serve pureed cauliflower alongside grilled steak.

- **Nutritional values:**
    - Calories: 450 kcal
    - Protein: 40 g
    - Carbohydrates: 10 g
    - Fat: 30 g

Vegetable Frittata with Low-Fat Cheese

- **Preparation time (P.T.):** 20 minutes
- **Ingredients (Ingr.):**
    - 6 eggs (approximately 300 g)

- 150 g bell pepper, diced

- 100 g spinach, chopped

- 50 g low-fat cheese, shredded

- 15 ml olive oil

- Salt and pepper to taste

- **Servings (Serves):** 2

- **Mode of cooking:** Stovetop

- **Procedure:**

1. Beat the eggs in a bowl with a dash of pepper and salt.

2. In a pan over medium heat, preheat the olive oil. Cook the spinach and bell pepper until they are tender.

3. Add the eggs to the pan and cook them until they set. Next, fold the frittata in half and sprinkle with cheese.

4. Serve right away.

- **Nutritional values:**

  - Calories: 300 kcal

  - Protein: 25 g

  - Carbohydrates: 10 g

  - Fat: 20 g

CHAPTER 6: RECOVERY DAY RECIPES

Chicken Salad with Avocado and Mango

- **Preparation time (P.T.):** 15 minutes

- **Ingredients (Ingr.):**

  o 200 g cooked chicken breast, diced

  o 1 avocado, diced (approximately 150 g)

  o 1 mango, diced (approximately 200 g)

  o 100 g cherry tomatoes, halved

  o 30 g red onion, thinly sliced

  o 30 ml olive oil

  o 15 ml lime juice

  o Salt and pepper to taste

- **Servings (Serves):** 2

- **Mode of cooking:** No cooking required

- **Procedure:**

1. Combine chicken, cherry tomatoes, avocado, mango, and red onion in a big bowl.

2. Combine lime juice and olive oil in a small bowl. Add pepper and salt for seasoning.

3. Pour the salad with the dressing and toss to mix.

4. Serve right away.

Nutritional values:

  o Calories: 350 kcal

  o Protein: 25 g

  o Carbohydrates: 25 g

  o Fat: 20 g

Turkey Meatloaf with Roasted Vegetables

- **Preparation time (P.T.):** 50 minutes

- **Ingredients (Ingr.):**

  o 400 g ground turkey

  o 50 g breadcrumbs

  o 1 egg (50 g)

  o 1 onion, diced (approximately 150 g)

  o 2 cloves garlic, minced (10 g)

  o 1 carrot, diced (approximately 100 g)

  o 1 bell pepper, diced (approximately 150 g)

  o 30 ml olive oil

  o 1 tsp dried thyme (2 g)

- 1 tsp dried rosemary (2 g)

  - Salt and pepper to taste

- **Servings (Serves):** 4

- **Mode of cooking:** Oven

- **Procedure:**

1. Set oven temperature to 190°C/375°F.

2. Combine the ground turkey, breadcrumbs, egg, garlic, thyme, rosemary, half of the diced onion, salt, and pepper in a big bowl. Mix thoroughly and shape into a loaf.

3. Transfer the meatloaf to an ovenproof dish.

4. Combine olive oil, salt, and pepper with the leftover onion, carrot, and bell pepper. Cover the meatloaf in the baking dish with it.

5. Bake for 40 minutes, or until vegetables are soft and meatloaf is thoroughly cooked.

6. Present right away.

Nutritional values:

  - Calories: 400 kcal

  - Protein: 30 g

  - Carbohydrates: 20 g

  - Fat: 20 g

Chocolate Banana Protein Smoothie

- **Preparation time (P.T.):** 5 minutes

- **Ingredients (Ingr.):**

  - 1 banana (approximately 120 g)

  - 30 g chocolate protein powder

  - 250 ml almond milk

  - 1 tsp cocoa powder (optional)

  - 1 tsp honey (optional)

- **Servings (Serves):** 1

- **Mode of cooking:** Blender

- **Procedure:**

1. Fill a blender with all the ingredients.

2. Purée until silky.

3. Transfer into a glass and serve right away.

Nutritional values:

  - Calories: 250 kcal

  - Protein: 20 g

  - Carbohydrates: 30 g

  - Fat: 5 g

Tuna Salad with Chickpeas and Peppers

- **Preparation time (P.T.):** 15 minutes

- **Ingredients (Ingr.):**

    o 200 g canned tuna, drained

    o 150 g chickpeas, rinsed and drained

    o 150 g bell pepper, diced

    o 100 g cherry tomatoes, halved

    o 30 g red onion, thinly sliced

    o 30 ml olive oil

    o 15 ml lemon juice

    o Salt and pepper to taste

- **Servings (Serves):** 2

- **Mode of cooking:** No cooking required

- **Procedure:**

1. Put the bell pepper, cherry tomatoes, red onion, chickpeas, and tuna in a big bowl.

2. Combine lemon juice and olive oil in a small bowl. Add pepper and salt for seasoning.

3. Pour the salad with the dressing and toss to mix.

4. Serve right away.

Nutritional values:

    o Calories: 300 kcal

    o Protein: 25 g

    o Carbohydrates: 20 g

    o Fat: 15 g

Grilled Chicken with Spinach and Strawberry Salad

- **Preparation time (P.T.):** 20 minutes

- **Ingredients (Ingr.):**

    o 2 chicken breasts (approximately 300 g)

    o 200 g spinach, washed and chopped

    o 150 g strawberries, sliced

    o 50 g feta cheese, crumbled

    o 30 g red onion, thinly sliced

    o 30 ml olive oil

    o 15 ml balsamic vinegar

    o Salt and pepper to taste

- **Servings (Serves):** 2

- **Mode of cooking:** Grill

- **Procedure:**

1. Turn the grill's heat up to medium-high.

2. Season chicken breasts with salt and pepper after brushing them with olive oil. Cook on the grill for 7–8 minutes on each side, or until well done.

3. Combine spinach, red onion, feta cheese, and strawberries in a big bowl.

4. Combine the olive oil and balsamic vinegar in a small basin. Add pepper and salt for seasoning.

5. Pour the salad with the dressing and toss to mix.

6. Present the spinach and strawberry salad alongside the cooked chicken.

Nutritional values:

- Calories: 350 kcal

- Protein: 35 g

- Carbohydrates: 20 g

- Fat: 15 g

Coffee and Almond Milk Protein Smoothie

- **Preparation time (P.T.):** 5 minutes

- **Ingredients (Ingr.):**

  - 250 ml cold brewed coffee

  - 30 g vanilla protein powder

  - 250 ml almond milk

  - 1 tsp honey (optional)

- **Servings (Serves):** 1

- **Mode of cooking:** Blender

- **Procedure:**

1. Fill a blender with all the ingredients.

2. Purée until silky.

3. Transfer into a glass and serve right away.

Nutritional values:

- Calories: 200 kcal

- Protein: 20 g

- Carbohydrates: 15 g

- Fat: 5 g

Cod Fillet with Sweet Potatoes and Green Beans

- **Preparation time (P.T.):** 25 minutes

- **Ingredients (Ingr.):**

  o 2 cod fillets (approximately 200 g each)

  o 400 g sweet potatoes, diced

  o 200 g green beans, trimmed

  o 30 ml olive oil

  o 1 tsp garlic powder (5 g)

  o Salt and pepper to taste

- **Servings (Serves):** 2

- **Mode of cooking:** Oven and stovetop

- **Procedure:**

1. Set oven temperature to 190°C/375°F.

2. Combine salt, pepper, garlic powder, and olive oil with sweet potatoes. Place on a baking pan, then bake until soft, about 25 minutes.

3. In the interim, sprinkle salt and pepper on the fish fillets. Transfer to a baking sheet and heat for 10 to 12 minutes, or until well done.

4. Cook green beans until they are soft.

5. Present baked cod alongside green beans and sweet potatoes.

Nutritional values:

  o Calories: 350 kcal

  o Protein: 30 g

  o Carbohydrates: 40 g

  o Fat: 10 g

Vegetable Omelet with Low-Fat Cheese

- **Preparation time (P.T.):** 15 minutes

- **Ingredients (Ingr.):**

  o 4 eggs (approximately 200 g)

  o 100 g bell pepper, diced

  o 100 g mushrooms, sliced

  o 50 g low-fat cheese, shredded

  o 15 ml olive oil

  o Salt and pepper to taste

- **Servings (Serves):** 2

- **Mode of cooking:** Stovetop

- **Procedure:**

1. Beat the eggs in a bowl with a dash of pepper and salt.

2. In a pan over medium heat, preheat the olive oil. When the mushrooms and bell pepper are soft, add them and simmer.

3. Add the eggs to the pan and cook them until they set. After adding some cheese, fold the omelet in half.

4. Serve right away.

Nutritional values:

- o Calories: 250 kcal

- o Protein: 20 g

- o Carbohydrates: 5 g

- o Fat: 18 g

Chicken Soup with Vegetables

- **Preparation time (P.T.):** 45 minutes

- **Ingredients (Ingr.):**

  - o 300 g chicken breast, cubed

  - o 150 g carrots, sliced

  - o 150 g celery, sliced

  - o 100 g onion, diced

  - o 2 cloves garlic, minced (10 g)

  - o 1 liter chicken broth

  - o 200 g spinach, washed and chopped

  - o 15 ml olive oil

  - o Salt and pepper to taste

- **Servings (Serves):** 4

- **Mode of cooking:** Stovetop

- **Procedure:**

1. In a big pot over medium heat, warm the olive oil. Add the garlic and onion and sauté until tender.

2. Cook the chicken until it turns brown.

3. Include the chicken broth, carrots, and celery. After reaching a boil, lower the heat, and simmer for 30 minutes.

4. Add the spinach and simmer for a further five minutes.

5. Season to taste with salt and pepper.

6. Present warm.

Nutritional values:

- o Calories: 250 kcal

- o Protein: 25 g

- o Carbohydrates: 15 g

- o Fat: 10 g

Egg Salad with Avocado and Spinach

- **Preparation time (P.T.):** 10 minutes

- **Ingredients (Ingr.):**

  - 4 boiled eggs, chopped (approximately 200 g)

  - 1 avocado, diced (approximately 150 g)

  - 100 g spinach, chopped

  - 30 ml Greek yogurt

  - 15 ml lemon juice

  - Salt and pepper to taste

- **Servings (Serves):** 2

- **Mode of cooking:** No cooking required

- **Procedure:**

1. Put spinach, avocado, and hard-boiled eggs in a big bowl.

2. Combine Greek yogurt, lemon juice, salt, and pepper in a small bowl.

3. Include the salad in the dressing and toss to mix.

4. Serve right away.

Nutritional values:

  - Calories: 300 kcal

  - Protein: 20 g

  - Carbohydrates: 10 g

  - Fat: 20 g

Grilled Chicken with Cabbage and Carrot Salad

- **Preparation time (P.T.):** 20 minutes

- **Ingredients (Ingr.):**

  - 2 chicken breasts (approximately 300 g)

  - 200 g cabbage, shredded

  - 100 g carrots, grated

  - 30 ml olive oil

  - 15 ml apple cider vinegar

  - Salt and pepper to taste

- **Servings (Serves):** 2

- **Mode of cooking:** Grill and no cooking required

- **Procedure:**

1. Turn the grill's heat up to medium-high.

2. Season chicken breasts with salt and pepper after brushing them with olive oil. Cook on the grill for 7–8 minutes on each side, or until well done.

3. Combine the carrots and cabbage in a big basin.

4. Combine apple cider vinegar and olive oil in a small basin. Add pepper and salt for seasoning.

5. Pour the salad with the dressing and toss to mix.

6. Present the grilled chicken beside a carrot salad and cabbage.

Nutritional values:

- Calories: 300 kcal
- Protein: 35 g
- Carbohydrates: 10 g
- Fat: 15 g

Egg White Frittata with Spinach and Green Onions

- **Preparation time (P.T.):** 15 minutes
- **Ingredients (Ingr.):**
  - 6 egg whites (approximately 200 g)
  - 100 g spinach, chopped
  - 50 g green onions, sliced
  - 15 ml olive oil
  - Salt and pepper to taste
- **Servings (Serves):** 2
- **Mode of cooking:** Stovetop
- **Procedure:**

1. Beat egg whites in a bowl with a dash of pepper and salt.

2. In a pan over medium heat, preheat the olive oil. When the spinach and green onions are soft, add them and simmer.

3. Add the egg whites to the pan and simmer, stirring periodically, until set.

4. Serve right away.

Nutritional values:

- Calories: 150 kcal
- Protein: 20 g
- Carbohydrates: 5 g
- Fat: 5 g

Tuna Salad with Green Beans and Olives

- **Preparation time (P.T.):** 15 minutes

- **Ingredients (Ingr.):**

  - 200 g canned tuna, drained

  - 150 g green beans, trimmed and blanched

  - 50 g black olives, sliced

  - 100 g cherry tomatoes, halved

  - 30 g red onion, thinly sliced

  - 30 ml olive oil

  - 15 ml lemon juice

  - Salt and pepper to taste

- **Servings (Serves):** 2

- **Mode of cooking:** No cooking required

- **Procedure:**

1. Put the tuna, green beans, cherry tomatoes, olives, and red onion in a big bowl.

2. Combine lemon juice and olive oil in a small bowl. Add pepper and salt for seasoning.

3. Pour the salad with the dressing and toss to mix.

4. Serve right away.

Nutritional values:

- Calories: 300 kcal

- Protein: 25 g

- Carbohydrates: 10 g

- Fat: 20 g

Grilled Chicken with Yogurt and Cucumber Sauce

- **Preparation time (P.T.):** 25 minutes

- **Ingredients (Ingr.):**

  - 2 chicken breasts (approximately 300 g)

  - 30 ml olive oil

  - 200 g Greek yogurt

  - 1 cucumber, grated (approximately 200 g)

  - 1 clove garlic, minced (5 g)

  - 15 ml lemon juice

  - 1 tsp dried dill (2 g)

  - Salt and pepper to taste

- **Servings (Serves):** 2
- **Mode of cooking:** Grill and no cooking required
- **Procedure:**

1. Turn the grill's heat up to medium-high.

2. Season chicken breasts with salt and pepper after brushing them with olive oil. Cook on the grill for 7–8 minutes on each side, or until well done.

3. Combine Greek yogurt, grated cucumber, dill, lemon juice, garlic, and salt and pepper in a small bowl.

4. Present the grilled chicken together with cucumber sauce and yogurt.

Nutritional values:

- Calories: 300 kcal
- Protein: 35 g
- Carbohydrates: 10 g
- Fat: 15 g

Vanilla Strawberry Protein Smoothie

- **Preparation time (P.T.):** 5 minutes
- **Ingredients (Ingr.):**
  - 150 g strawberries, hulled
  - 30 g vanilla protein powder
  - 250 ml almond milk
  - 1 tsp honey (optional)
- **Servings (Serves):** 1
- **Mode of cooking:** Blender
- **Procedure:**

1. Fill a blender with all the ingredients.

2. Purée until silky.

3. Transfer into a glass and serve right away.

Nutritional values:

- Calories: 200 kcal
- Protein: 20 g
- Carbohydrates: 20 g
- Fat: 5 g

Baked Cod with Sweet Potatoes and Spinach

- **Preparation time (P.T.):** 30 minutes
- **Ingredients (Ingr.):**
  - 2 cod fillets (approximately 200 g each)
  - 400 g sweet potatoes, diced

- o 200 g spinach, washed and chopped

- o 30 ml olive oil

- o 1 tsp garlic powder (5 g)

- o Salt and pepper to taste

- **Servings (Serves):** 2

- **Mode of cooking:** Oven and stovetop

- **Procedure:**

1. Set oven temperature to 190°C/375°F.

2. Combine salt, pepper, garlic powder, and olive oil with sweet potatoes. Place on a baking pan, then bake until soft, about 25 minutes.

3. In the interim, sprinkle salt and pepper on the fish fillets. Transfer to a baking sheet and heat for 10 to 12 minutes, or until well done.

4. Cook spinach in steam until it wilts.

5. Present cooked cod alongside spinach and sweet potatoes.

Nutritional values:

- o Calories: 350 kcal

- o Protein: 30 g

- o Carbohydrates: 40 g

- o Fat: 10 g

Paprika Chicken with Grilled Vegetables

- **Preparation time (P.T.):** 30 minutes

- **Ingredients (Ingr.):**

  - o 2 chicken breasts (approximately 300 g)

  - o 1 bell pepper, sliced (approximately 150 g)

  - o 1 zucchini, sliced (approximately 200 g)

  - o 1 red onion, sliced (approximately 100 g)

  - o 30 ml olive oil

  - o 1 tsp paprika (5 g)

  - o Salt and pepper to taste

- **Servings (Serves):** 2

- **Mode of cooking:** Grill and stovetop

- **Procedure:**

1. Turn the grill's heat up to medium-high.

2. Combine the olive oil, paprika, salt, and pepper in a small bowl.

3. Grill the chicken breasts for 7 to 8 minutes on each side, or until they are

cooked through, after brushing them with the mixture.

4. Toss the red onion, zucchini, and bell pepper slices with the leftover olive oil and grill until soft.

5. Serve the grilled veggies alongside the chicken breast.

Nutritional values:

- Calories: 400 kcal

- Protein: 35 g

- Carbohydrates: 10 g

- Fat: 20 g

Red Pepper and Onion Frittata

- **Preparation time (P.T.):** 20 minutes

- **Ingredients (Ingr.):**

  - 6 eggs (approximately 300 g)

  - 150 g red bell pepper, diced

  - 100 g onion, diced

  - 15 ml olive oil

  - Salt and pepper to taste

- **Servings (Serves):** 2

- **Mode of cooking:** Stovetop

- **Procedure:**

1. Beat the eggs in a bowl with a dash of pepper and salt.

2. In a pan over medium heat, preheat the olive oil. When the onion and red bell pepper are soft, add them and simmer.

3. Add the eggs to the pan and cook them until they set. Serve the frittata right away after folding it in half.

Nutritional values:

- Calories: 250 kcal

- Protein: 20 g

- Carbohydrates: 5 g

- Fat: 18 g

Shrimp Salad with Avocado and Lime

- **Preparation time (P.T.):** 15 minutes

- **Ingredients (Ingr.):**

  - 200 g cooked shrimp

  - 1 avocado, diced (approximately 150 g)

  - 100 g cherry tomatoes, halved

  - 30 g red onion, thinly sliced

- o   30 ml olive oil

- o   15 ml lime juice

- o   Salt and pepper to taste

- **Servings (Serves):** 2

- **Mode of cooking:** No cooking required

- **Procedure:**

1. Put the shrimp, avocado, cherry tomatoes, and red onion in a big bowl.

2. Combine lime juice and olive oil in a small bowl. Add pepper and salt for seasoning.

3. Pour the salad with the dressing and toss to mix.

4. Serve right away.

Nutritional values:

- o   Calories: 350 kcal

- o   Protein: 25 g

- o   Carbohydrates: 15 g

- o   Fat: 20 g

Chicken Curry with Basmati Rice

- **Preparation time (P.T.):** 35 minutes

- **Ingredients (Ingr.):**

  - o   300 g chicken breast, cubed

  - o   200 g Greek yogurt

  - o   30 g curry powder

  - o   1 onion, diced (approximately 150 g)

  - o   2 cloves garlic, minced (10 g)

  - o   400 g diced tomatoes (canned)

  - o   200 ml coconut milk

  - o   180 g basmati rice

  - o   15 ml olive oil

  - o   Salt and pepper to taste

- **Servings (Serves):** 2

- **Mode of cooking:** Stovetop

- **Procedure:**

1. Combine the chicken, Greek yogurt, and curry powder in a bowl. For a minimum of half an hour, marinate.

2. Prepare basmati rice as directed on the package.

3. In a pan over medium heat, preheat the olive oil. Add the garlic and onion, and cook until transparent.

4. Cook the marinated chicken until it turns golden brown on all sides.

5. Stir in the coconut milk and diced tomatoes. Once the chicken is cooked through, reduce heat to a simmer and cook for 15 to 20 minutes.

6. Spoon curry chicken over basmati rice.

Nutritional values:

- Calories: 500 kcal

- Protein: 35 g

- Carbohydrates: 50 g

- Fat: 20 g

Chicken Salad with Almonds and Grapes

- **Preparation time (P.T.):** 15 minutes

- **Ingredients (Ingr.):**

  - 200 g cooked chicken breast, diced

  - 50 g almonds, sliced

  - 150 g grapes, halved

  - 100 g celery, diced

  - 50 g Greek yogurt

  - 15 ml lemon juice

  - Salt and pepper to taste

- **Servings (Serves):** 2

- **Mode of cooking:** No cooking required

- **Procedure:**

1. Combine the chicken, celery, grapes, and almonds in a big bowl.

2. Combine Greek yogurt, lemon juice, salt, and pepper in a small bowl.

3. Include the salad in the dressing and toss to mix.

4. Serve right away.

Nutritional values:

- Calories: 300 kcal

- Protein: 25 g

- Carbohydrates: 20 g

- Fat: 15 g

Mixed Berry Protein Smoothie

- **Preparation time (P.T.):** 5 minutes

- **Ingredients (Ingr.):**

  - 100 g mixed berries (strawberries, blueberries, raspberries)

  - 30 g vanilla protein powder

  - 250 ml almond milk

  - 1 tsp honey (optional)

- **Servings (Serves):** 1

- **Mode of cooking:** Blender

- **Procedure:**

1. Fill a blender with all the ingredients.

2. Purée until silky.

3. Transfer into a glass and serve right away.

Nutritional values:

  - Calories: 200 kcal

  - Protein: 20 g

  - Carbohydrates: 25 g

  - Fat: 5 g

Oven-Roasted Turkey with Steamed Vegetables

- **Preparation time (P.T.):** 45 minutes

- **Ingredients (Ingr.):**

  - 400 g turkey breast, sliced

  - 30 ml olive oil

  - 1 tsp dried thyme (2 g)

  - 1 tsp garlic powder (5 g)

  - 200 g broccoli florets

  - 200 g carrots, sliced

  - Salt and pepper to taste

- **Servings (Serves):** 2

- **Mode of cooking:** Oven and stovetop

- **Procedure:**

1. Set oven temperature to 190°C/375°F.

2. Apply salt, pepper, garlic powder, thyme, and olive oil to the turkey breast.

3. Bake for 35 to 40 minutes, or until thoroughly done, for roasting.

4. In the interim, simmer carrots and broccoli until they are soft.

5. Present the cooked turkey alongside steaming veggies.

Nutritional values:

- o Calories: 350 kcal
- o Protein: 30 g
- o Carbohydrates: 15 g
- o Fat: 15 g

Kale Salad with Avocado and Pumpkin Seeds

- **Preparation time (P.T.):** 10 minutes
- **Ingredients (Ingr.):**
  - o 150 g kale, chopped
  - o 1 avocado, diced (approximately 150 g)
  - o 30 g pumpkin seeds
  - o 100 g cherry tomatoes, halved
  - o 30 ml olive oil
  - o 15 ml lemon juice
  - o Salt and pepper to taste
- **Servings (Serves):** 2
- **Mode of cooking:** No cooking required

- **Procedure:**

1. Combine the kale, avocado, pumpkin seeds, and cherry tomatoes in a big bowl.

2. Combine lemon juice and olive oil in a small bowl. Add pepper and salt for seasoning.

3. Pour the salad with the dressing and toss to mix.

4. Serve right away.

Nutritional values:

- o Calories: 300 kcal
- o Protein: 10 g
- o Carbohydrates: 20 g
- o Fat: 20 g

Egg White Frittata with Peppers and Onions

- **Preparation time (P.T.):** 15 minutes
- **Ingredients (Ingr.):**
  - o 6 egg whites (approximately 200 g)
  - o 150 g bell pepper, diced
  - o 100 g onion, diced

o   15 ml olive oil

  o   Salt and pepper to taste

- **Servings (Serves):** 2

- **Mode of cooking:** Stovetop

- **Procedure:**

1. Beat egg whites in a bowl with a dash of pepper and salt.

2. In a pan over medium heat, preheat the olive oil. Add onion and bell pepper, and sauté until tender.

3. Add the egg whites to the pan and simmer, stirring periodically, until set.

4. Serve right away.

Nutritional values:

  o   Calories: 150 kcal

  o   Protein: 20 g

  o   Carbohydrates: 5 g

  o   Fat: 5 g

Chicken Curry with Brown Rice

- **Preparation time (P.T.):** 35 minutes

- **Ingredients (Ingr.):**

  o   300 g chicken breast, cubed

  o   200 g Greek yogurt

  o   30 g curry powder

  o   1 onion, diced (approximately 150 g)

  o   2 cloves garlic, minced (10 g)

  o   400 g diced tomatoes (canned)

  o   200 ml coconut milk

  o   180 g brown rice

  o   15 ml olive oil

  o   Salt and pepper to taste

- **Servings (Serves):** 2

- **Mode of cooking:** Stovetop

- **Procedure:**

1. Combine the chicken, Greek yogurt, and curry powder in a bowl. For a minimum of half an hour, marinate.

2. Prepare brown rice as directed on the package.

3. In a pan over medium heat, preheat the olive oil. Add the garlic and onion, and cook until transparent.

4. Cook the marinated chicken until it turns golden brown on all sides.

5. Stir in the coconut milk and diced tomatoes. Once the chicken is cooked

through, reduce heat to a simmer and cook for 15 to 20 minutes.

6. Spoon brown rice over chicken curry.

Nutritional values:

- o Calories: 500 kcal
- o Protein: 35 g
- o Carbohydrates: 50 g
- o Fat: 20 g

Tuna Salad with Black Beans and Corn

- **Preparation time (P.T.):** 15 minutes

- **Ingredients (Ingr.):**

  - o 200 g canned tuna, drained
  - o 150 g black beans, rinsed and drained
  - o 150 g corn kernels
  - o 100 g cherry tomatoes, halved
  - o 30 g red onion, thinly sliced
  - o 30 ml olive oil
  - o 15 ml lime juice
  - o Salt and pepper to taste

- **Servings (Serves):** 2

- **Mode of cooking:** No cooking required

- **Procedure:**

1. Combine the tuna, red onion, cherry tomatoes, black beans, and corn in a big bowl.

2. Combine lime juice and olive oil in a small bowl. Add pepper and salt for seasoning.

3. Pour the salad with the dressing and toss to mix.

4. Serve right away.

Nutritional values:

- o Calories: 350 kcal
- o Protein: 25 g
- o Carbohydrates: 30 g
- o Fat: 15 g

Grilled Chicken with Yogurt and Cucumber Sauce

- **Preparation time (P.T.):** 25 minutes

- **Ingredients (Ingr.):**

  - o 2 chicken breasts (approximately 300 g)

- 30 ml olive oil

- 200 g Greek yogurt

- 1 cucumber, grated (approximately 200 g)

- 1 clove garlic, minced (5 g)

- 15 ml lemon juice

- 1 tsp dried dill (2 g)

- Salt and pepper to taste

- **Servings (Serves):** 2

- **Mode of cooking:** Grill and no cooking required

- **Procedure:**

1. Set the grill's temperature to medium-high.

2. Add salt and pepper to the chicken breasts after brushing them with olive oil. Cook on the grill for 7 to 8 minutes on each side, or until done.

3. Combine Greek yogurt, dill, lemon juice, grated cucumber, garlic, salt, and pepper in a small bowl.

4. Present cucumber sauce and yogurt alongside grilled chicken.

Nutritional values:

- Calories: 300 kcal

- Protein: 35 g

- Carbohydrates: 10 g

- Fat: 15 g

Spinach and Sun-Dried Tomato Frittata

- **Preparation time (P.T.):** 20 minutes

- **Ingredients (Ingr.):**

  - 6 eggs (approximately 300 g)

  - 150 g spinach, chopped

  - 50 g sun-dried tomatoes, chopped

  - 50 g low-fat cheese, shredded

  - 15 ml olive oil

  - Salt and pepper to taste

- **Servings (Serves):** 2

- **Mode of cooking:** Stovetop

- **Procedure:**

1. Beat the eggs in a bowl with a dash of pepper and salt.

2. In a pan over medium heat, preheat the olive oil. Cook the spinach until it softens, then add the sun-dried tomatoes.

3. Add the eggs to the pan and cook them until they set. Next, fold the frittata in half and sprinkle with cheese.

4. Serve right away.

Nutritional values:

- o Calories: 300 kcal

- o Protein: 25 g

- o Carbohydrates: 10 g

- o Fat: 20 g

Shrimp Salad with Avocado and Lime

- **Preparation time (P.T.):** 15 minutes

- **Ingredients (Ingr.):**

  - o 200 g cooked shrimp

  - o 1 avocado, diced (approximately 150 g)

  - o 100 g cherry tomatoes, halved

  - o 30 g red onion, thinly sliced

  - o 30 ml olive oil

  - o 15 ml lime juice

  - o Salt and pepper to taste

- **Servings (Serves):** 2

- **Mode of cooking:** No cooking required

- **Procedure:**

1. Put the shrimp, avocado, cherry tomatoes, and red onion in a big bowl.

2. Combine lime juice and olive oil in a small bowl. Add pepper and salt for seasoning.

3. Pour the salad with the dressing and toss to mix.

4. Serve right away.

Nutritional values:

- o Calories: 350 kcal

- o Protein: 25 g

- o Carbohydrates: 15 g

- o Fat: 20 g

CHAPTER 7: VARIOUS RECIPES

Turkey Burger with Coleslaw

- **Preparation time (P.T.):** 25 minutes

- **Ingredients (Ingr.):**

  - 400 g ground turkey

  - 50 g breadcrumbs

  - 1 egg (50 g)

  - 1 tsp garlic powder (5 g)

  - 1 tsp onion powder (5 g)

  - 200 g cabbage, shredded

  - 100 g carrots, grated

  - 50 g Greek yogurt

  - 15 ml apple cider vinegar

  - 30 ml olive oil

  - Salt and pepper to taste

- **Servings (Serves):** 2

- **Mode of cooking:** Grill

- **Procedure:**

1. Combine the ground turkey, breadcrumbs, egg, onion and garlic powders, salt, and pepper in a bowl. Shape into patties.
2. Turn the grill's heat up to medium-high. Turkey patties should be cooked through after grilling for 5 to 6 minutes on each side, brushed with olive oil.
3. To make coleslaw, combine carrots, cabbage, Greek yogurt, apple cider vinegar, salt, and pepper in a separate bowl.
4. Present turkey burgers with a side order of coleslaw.

Nutritional values:

  - Calories: 400 kcal

  - Protein: 35 g

  - Carbohydrates: 20 g

  - Fat: 20 g

Chicken Curry with Cauliflower Rice

- **Preparation time (P.T.):** 30 minutes

- **Ingredients (Ingr.):**

  - 300 g chicken breast, cubed

  - 200 g Greek yogurt

  - 30 g curry powder

  - 1 onion, diced (approximately 150 g)

  - 2 cloves garlic, minced (10 g)

  - 400 g diced tomatoes (canned)

  - 200 ml coconut milk

- o 300 g cauliflower, riced

- o 15 ml olive oil

- o Salt and pepper to taste

- **Servings (Serves):** 2

- **Mode of cooking:** Stovetop

- **Procedure:**

1. Combine the chicken, Greek yogurt, and curry powder in a bowl. For a minimum of half an hour, marinate.
2. In a pan over medium heat, preheat the olive oil. Add the garlic and onion, and cook until transparent.
3. Cook the marinated chicken until it turns golden brown on all sides.
4. Stir in the coconut milk and diced tomatoes. Once the chicken is cooked through, reduce heat to a simmer and cook for 15 to 20 minutes.
5. In the interim, steam the cauliflower rice until it's soft.
6. Toss with cauliflower rice and serve chicken curry.

Nutritional values:

- o Calories: 400 kcal

- o Protein: 35 g

- o Carbohydrates: 20 g

- o Fat: 20 g

Egg White Frittata with Zucchini and Onions

- **Preparation time (P.T.):** 15 minutes

- **Ingredients (Ingr.):**

  - o 6 egg whites (approximately 200 g)

  - o 150 g zucchini, diced

  - o 100 g onion, diced

  - o 15 ml olive oil

  - o Salt and pepper to taste

- **Servings (Serves):** 2

- **Mode of cooking:** Stovetop

- **Procedure:**

1. Beat egg whites in a bowl with a dash of pepper and salt.
2. In a pan over medium heat, preheat the olive oil. Cook the onion and zucchini until they are tender.
3. Add the egg whites to the pan and simmer, stirring periodically, until set.
4. Serve right away.

Nutritional values:

- o Calories: 150 kcal

- o Protein: 20 g

o Carbohydrates: 5 g

o Fat: 5 g

Shrimp Salad with Avocado and Lime

- **Preparation time (P.T.):** 15 minutes

- **Ingredients (Ingr.):**

  o 200 g cooked shrimp

  o 1 avocado, diced (approximately 150 g)

  o 100 g cherry tomatoes, halved

  o 30 g red onion, thinly sliced

  o 30 ml olive oil

  o 15 ml lime juice

  o Salt and pepper to taste

- **Servings (Serves):** 2

- **Mode of cooking:** No cooking required

- **Procedure:**

1. In a big bowl, mix together shrimp, avocado, cherry tomatoes, and red onion.
2. Combine lime juice and olive oil in a small bowl. Add pepper and salt for seasoning.
3. Pour the salad with the dressing and toss to mix.
4. Serve right away.

Nutritional values:

  o Calories: 350 kcal

  o Protein: 25 g

  o Carbohydrates: 15 g

  o Fat: 20 g

Vanilla Strawberry Protein Smoothie

- **Preparation time (P.T.):** 5 minutes

- **Ingredients (Ingr.):**

  o 150 g strawberries, hulled

  o 30 g vanilla protein powder

  o 250 ml almond milk

  o 1 tsp honey (optional)

- **Servings (Serves):** 1

- **Mode of cooking:** Blender

- **Procedure:**

1. Fill a blender with all the ingredients.
2. Purée until silky.
3. Transfer into a glass and serve right away.

Nutritional values:

  o Calories: 200 kcal

- Protein: 20 g
- Carbohydrates: 20 g
- Fat: 5 g

Beef Steak with Arugula and Parmesan Salad

- **Preparation time (P.T.):** 20 minutes
- **Ingredients (Ingr.):**
  - 2 beef steaks (approximately 200 g each)
  - 30 ml olive oil
  - 100 g arugula
  - 50 g Parmesan cheese, shaved
  - 15 ml lemon juice
  - Salt and pepper to taste
- **Servings (Serves):** 2
- **Mode of cooking:** Grill and no cooking required
- **Procedure:**

1. Turn the heat up to medium-high on the grill.
2. Season steaks with salt and pepper after brushing them with olive oil. Grill for 5 to 7 minutes on each side, or until done to taste.
3. Combine the arugula and Parmesan cheese in a big basin.
4. Combine the lemon juice and olive oil in a small bowl. Add pepper and salt for seasoning.
5. Pour the salad with the dressing and toss to mix.
6. Present arugula and Parmesan salad alongside the grilled steak.

Nutritional values:

- Calories: 450 kcal
- Protein: 35 g
- Carbohydrates: 5 g
- Fat: 30 g

Chicken Meatballs with Yogurt Sauce

- **Preparation time (P.T.):** 30 minutes
- **Ingredients (Ingr.):**
  - 400 g ground chicken
  - 50 g breadcrumbs
  - 1 egg (50 g)
  - 1 onion, diced (approximately 150 g)
  - 2 cloves garlic, minced (10 g)
  - 200 g Greek yogurt

- o 1 cucumber, grated (approximately 200 g)

- o 1 clove garlic, minced (5 g)

- o 15 ml lemon juice

- o Salt and pepper to taste

- **Servings (Serves):** 4

- **Mode of cooking:** Oven and no cooking required

- **Procedure:**

1. Set oven temperature to 190°C/375°F.
2. In a large bowl, mix together the ground chicken, breadcrumbs, egg, garlic, half of the diced onion, salt, and pepper. Stir thoroughly and shape into meatballs.
3. After the meatballs are placed on a baking sheet, bake them for 20 to 25 minutes, or until done.
4. To make the yogurt sauce, put the Greek yogurt, grated cucumber, garlic, lemon juice, salt, and pepper in a small bowl.
5. Serve yogurt sauce over chicken meatballs.

Nutritional values:

- o Calories: 300 kcal

- o Protein: 25 g

- o Carbohydrates: 15 g

- o Fat: 15 g

Tuna Salad with Black Beans and Corn

- **Preparation time (P.T.):** 15 minutes

- **Ingredients (Ingr.):**

  - o 200 g canned tuna, drained

  - o 150 g black beans, rinsed and drained

  - o 150 g corn kernels

  - o 100 g cherry tomatoes, halved

  - o 30 g red onion, thinly sliced

  - o 30 ml olive oil

  - o 15 ml lime juice

  - o Salt and pepper to taste

- **Servings (Serves):** 2

- **Mode of cooking:** No cooking required

- **Procedure:**

1. In a big bowl, mix together tuna, black beans, corn, cherry tomatoes, and red onion.
2. Combine lime juice and olive oil in a small bowl. Add pepper and salt for seasoning.
3. Pour the salad with the dressing and toss

to mix.

4. Serve right away.

Nutritional values:

- Calories: 350 kcal
- Protein: 25 g
- Carbohydrates: 30 g
- Fat: 15 g

Grilled Chicken with Avocado Sauce

- **Preparation time (P.T.):** 20 minutes

- **Ingredients (Ingr.):**

  - 2 chicken breasts (approximately 300 g)
  - 1 avocado, mashed (approximately 150 g)
  - 30 ml Greek yogurt
  - 15 ml lime juice
  - 1 clove garlic, minced (5 g)
  - 30 ml olive oil
  - Salt and pepper to taste

- **Servings (Serves):** 2

- **Mode of cooking:** Grill and no cooking required

- **Procedure:**

1. Turn the heat up to medium-high on the grill.
2. Season chicken breasts with salt and pepper after brushing them with olive oil. Cook on the grill for 7–8 minutes on each side, or until done.
3. Combine Greek yogurt, mashed avocado, lime juice, garlic, salt, and pepper in a small bowl.
4. Present avocado sauce beside grilled chicken.

Nutritional values:

- Calories: 350 kcal
- Protein: 35 g
- Carbohydrates: 10 g
- Fat: 20 g

Spinach Frittata with Goat Cheese

- **Preparation time (P.T.):** 20 minutes

- **Ingredients (Ingr.):**

  - 6 eggs (approximately 300 g)
  - 150 g spinach, chopped
  - 50 g goat cheese, crumbled
  - 15 ml olive oil

o Salt and pepper to taste

- **Servings (Serves):** 2

- **Mode of cooking:** Stovetop

- **Procedure:**

1. Beat the eggs in a bowl with a dash of pepper and salt.
2. In a pan over medium heat, preheat the olive oil. When the spinach begins to wilt, add it.
3. Add the eggs to the pan and cook them until they set. Fold the frittata in half and sprinkle the goat cheese on top.
4. Serve right away.

Nutritional values:

o Calories: 300 kcal

o Protein: 25 g

o Carbohydrates: 5 g

o Fat: 20 g

Chicken Curry with Basmati Rice

- **Preparation time (P.T.):** 35 minutes

- **Ingredients (Ingr.):**

o 300 g chicken breast, cubed

o 200 g Greek yogurt

o 30 g curry powder

o 1 onion, diced (approximately 150 g)

o 2 cloves garlic, minced (10 g)

o 400 g diced tomatoes (canned)

o 200 ml coconut milk

o 180 g basmati rice

o 15 ml olive oil

o Salt and pepper to taste

- **Servings (Serves):** 2

- **Mode of cooking:** Stovetop

- **Procedure:**

1. In a bowl, mix the chicken, Greek yogurt, and curry powder. For a minimum of half an hour, marinate.
2. Prepare basmati rice as directed on the package.
3. In a pan over medium heat, preheat the olive oil. Add the garlic and onion, and cook until transparent.
4. Cook the marinated chicken until it turns golden brown on all sides.
5. Stir in the coconut milk and diced tomatoes. Once the chicken is cooked through, reduce heat to a simmer and cook for 15 to 20 minutes.
6. Spoon curry chicken over basmati rice.

Nutritional values:

- o Calories: 500 kcal
- o Protein: 35 g
- o Carbohydrates: 50 g
- o Fat: 20 g

Tuna Salad with Black Beans and Corn

- **Preparation time (P.T.):** 15 minutes
- **Ingredients (Ingr.):**
  - o 200 g canned tuna, drained
  - o 150 g black beans, rinsed and drained
  - o 150 g corn kernels
  - o 100 g cherry tomatoes, halved
  - o 30 g red onion, thinly sliced
  - o 30 ml olive oil
  - o 15 ml lime juice
  - o Salt and pepper to taste
- **Servings (Serves):** 2
- **Mode of cooking:** No cooking required

- **Procedure:**

1. Put the tuna, red onion, cherry tomatoes, black beans, and corn in a big bowl.
2. Combine olive oil and lime juice in a small bowl. Use pepper and salt for seasoning.
3. Pour the salad with the dressing and mix to incorporate.
4. Start serving right away.

Nutritional values:

- o Calories: 350 kcal
- o Protein: 25 g
- o Carbohydrates: 30 g
- o Fat: 15 g

Grilled Chicken with Yogurt and Cucumber Sauce

- **Preparation time (P.T.):** 25 minutes
- **Ingredients (Ingr.):**
  - o 2 chicken breasts (approximately 300 g)
  - o 30 ml olive oil
  - o 200 g Greek yogurt
  - o 1 cucumber, grated (approximately 200 g)

o 1 clove garlic, minced (5 g)

o 15 ml lemon juice

o 1 tsp dried dill (2 g)

o Salt and pepper to taste

- **Servings (Serves):** 2

- **Mode of cooking:** Grill and no cooking required

- **Procedure:**

1. Turn the heat up to medium-high on the grill.

2. Season chicken breasts with salt and pepper after brushing them with olive oil. Cook on the grill for 7–8 minutes on each side, or until done.

3. In a small bowl, mix together Greek yogurt, grated cucumber, garlic, lemon juice, dill, salt, and pepper.

4. Present the grilled chicken together with cucumber sauce and yogurt.

Nutritional values:

o Calories: 300 kcal

o Protein: 35 g

o Carbohydrates: 10 g

o Fat: 15 g

Spinach and Sun-Dried Tomato Frittata

- **Preparation time (P.T.):** 20 minutes

- **Ingredients (Ingr.):**

o 6 eggs (approximately 300 g)

o 150 g spinach, chopped

o 50 g sun-dried tomatoes, chopped

o 50 g low-fat cheese, shredded

o 15 ml olive oil

o Salt and pepper to taste

- **Servings (Serves):** 2

- **Mode of cooking:** Stovetop

- **Procedure:**

1. Beat the eggs with a dash of pepper and salt in a bowl.

2. In a pan, warm the olive oil over medium heat. Cook until softened, then add the spinach and sun-dried tomatoes.

3. Add eggs to the pan and heat until solidified. After folding the frittata in half, sprinkle cheese on top.

4. Present right away.

Nutritional values:

- Calories: 300 kcal
- Protein: 25 g
- Carbohydrates: 10 g
- Fat: 20 g

Shrimp Salad with Avocado and Lime

- **Preparation time (P.T.):** 15 minutes

- **Ingredients (Ingr.):**

  - 200 g cooked shrimp
  - 1 avocado, diced (approximately 150 g)
  - 100 g cherry tomatoes, halved
  - 30 g red onion, thinly sliced
  - 30 ml olive oil
  - 15 ml lime juice
  - Salt and pepper to taste

- **Servings (Serves):** 2

- **Mode of cooking:** No cooking required

- **Procedure:**

1. In a big bowl, mix together shrimp, avocado, cherry tomatoes, and red onion.
2. Combine lime juice and olive oil in a small bowl. Add pepper and salt for seasoning.
3. Pour the salad with the dressing and toss to mix.
4. Serve right away.

Nutritional values:

- Calories: 350 kcal
- Protein: 25 g
- Carbohydrates: 15 g
- Fat: 20 g

Chocolate Mint Protein Smoothie

- **Preparation time (P.T.):** 5 minutes

- **Ingredients (Ingr.):**

  - 1 banana (approximately 120 g)
  - 30 g chocolate protein powder
  - 250 ml almond milk
  - 10 mint leaves
  - 1 tsp cocoa powder (optional)
  - 1 tsp honey (optional)

- **Servings (Serves):** 1

- **Mode of cooking:** Blender

- **Procedure:**

1. Fill a blender with all the ingredients.
2. Purée until silky.
3. Transfer into a glass and serve right away.

Nutritional values:

- o Calories: 250 kcal
- o Protein: 20 g
- o Carbohydrates: 30 g
- o Fat: 5 g

Almond-crusted cod with Broccoli

- **Preparation time (P.T.):** 25 minutes

- **Ingredients (Ingr.):**

  - o 2 cod fillets (approximately 200 g each)
  - o 50 g ground almonds
  - o 1 egg, beaten (50 g)
  - o 30 ml olive oil
  - o 300 g broccoli florets
  - o Salt and pepper to taste

- **Servings (Serves):** 2

- **Mode of cooking:** Oven and stovetop

- **Procedure:**

1. Set oven temperature to 190°C/375°F.
2. Coat the fish fillets with ground almonds after dipping them in the beaten egg.
3. In a pan over medium heat, preheat the olive oil. Brown all sides of the fish fillets.
4. Place the cod on a baking pan and cook it for ten minutes.
5. Cook broccoli in steam until soft.
6. Present cod coated in almonds alongside steaming broccoli.

Nutritional values:

- o Calories: 350 kcal
- o Protein: 30 g
- o Carbohydrates: 10 g
- o Fat: 20 g

Paprika Chicken with Sweet Potatoes

- **Preparation time (P.T.):** 40 minutes

- **Ingredients (Ingr.):**

  - o 2 chicken thighs (approximately 300 g)
  - o 400 g sweet potatoes, diced
  - o 30 ml olive oil
  - o 1 tsp paprika (5 g)

- o 1 tsp garlic powder (5 g)
- o Salt and pepper to taste

- **Servings (Serves):** 2

- **Mode of cooking:** Oven

- **Procedure:**

1. Set oven temperature to 200°C/400°F.
2. In a baking dish, combine sweet potatoes, olive oil, paprika, garlic powder, salt, and pepper.
3. After placing the chicken thighs over the sweet potatoes, season them with pepper and salt.
4. Bake for 35 to 40 minutes, or until the sweet potatoes are soft and the chicken is thoroughly cooked.
5. Present right away.

Nutritional values:

- o Calories: 500 kcal
- o Protein: 30 g
- o Carbohydrates: 45 g
- o Fat: 20 g

Egg White Frittata with Zucchini and Onions

- **Preparation time (P.T.):** 15 minutes

- **Ingredients (Ingr.):**

  - o 6 egg whites (approximately 200 g)
  - o 150 g zucchini, diced
  - o 100 g onion, diced
  - o 15 ml olive oil
  - o Salt and pepper to taste

- **Servings (Serves):** 2

- **Mode of cooking:** Stovetop

- **Procedure:**

1. In a bowl, whisk together egg whites with a dash of salt and pepper.
2. In a pan over medium heat, preheat the olive oil. Cook the onion and zucchini until they are tender.
3. Add the egg whites to the pan and simmer, stirring periodically, until set.
4. Serve right away.

Nutritional values:

- o Calories: 150 kcal
- o Protein: 20 g
- o Carbohydrates: 5 g
- o Fat: 5 g

Tuna Salad with Green Beans and Olives

- **Preparation time (P.T.):** 15 minutes

- **Ingredients (Ingr.):**

  - 200 g canned tuna, drained

  - 150 g green beans, trimmed and blanched

  - 50 g black olives, sliced

  - 100 g cherry tomatoes, halved

  - 30 g red onion, thinly sliced

  - 30 ml olive oil

  - 15 ml lemon juice

  - Salt and pepper to taste

- **Servings (Serves):** 2

- **Mode of cooking:** No cooking required

- **Procedure:**

1. In a big bowl, mix tuna, green beans, cherry tomatoes, olives, and red onion together.

2. Whisk lemon juice and olive oil together in a small bowl. Use pepper and salt for seasoning.

3. Pour the salad with the dressing and mix to incorporate.

4. Start serving right away.

Nutritional values:

  - Calories: 300 kcal

  - Protein: 25 g

  - Carbohydrates: 10 g

  - Fat: 20 g

Grilled Chicken with Lemon Herb Sauce

- **Preparation time (P.T.):** 20 minutes

- **Ingredients (Ingr.):**

  - 2 chicken breasts (approximately 300 g)

  - 30 ml olive oil

  - 1 lemon, juiced

  - 1 tsp dried thyme (2 g)

  - 1 tsp dried rosemary (2 g)

  - Salt and pepper to taste

- **Servings (Serves):** 2

- **Mode of cooking:** Grill

- **Procedure:**

1. Warm up the grill to a temperature of medium-high.

2. Combine lemon juice, olive oil,

rosemary, thyme, salt, and pepper in a small bowl.

3. Next, grill the chicken breasts for 7 to 8 minutes on each side, or until done. Brush them with the mixture.

4. Start serving right away.

Nutritional values:

- o Calories: 300 kcal

- o Protein: 35 g

- o Carbohydrates: 5 g

- o Fat: 15 g

Spinach and Mushroom Frittata

- • **Preparation time (P.T.):** 20 minutes

- • **Ingredients (Ingr.):**

  - o 6 eggs (approximately 300 g)

  - o 150 g spinach, chopped

  - o 150 g mushrooms, sliced

  - o 15 ml olive oil

  - o Salt and pepper to taste

- • **Servings (Serves):** 2

- • **Mode of cooking:** Stovetop

- • **Procedure:**

1. Beat the eggs in a bowl with a dash of pepper and salt.

2. In a pan over medium heat, preheat the olive oil. When the spinach and mushrooms are soft, add them and simmer.

3. Add the eggs to the pan and cook them until they set. Serve the frittata right away after folding it in half.

Nutritional values:

- o Calories: 250 kcal

- o Protein: 20 g

- o Carbohydrates: 5 g

- o Fat: 18 g

Grilled Salmon with Asparagus and Quinoa

- • **Preparation time (P.T.):** 25 minutes

- • **Ingredients (Ingr.):**

  - o 2 salmon fillets (approximately 200 g each)

  - o 450 g asparagus, trimmed

  - o 180 g quinoa

  - o 500 ml vegetable broth

  - o 30 ml olive oil

  - o Salt and pepper to taste

- **Servings (Serves):** 2
- **Mode of cooking:** Grill and stovetop
- **Procedure:**

1. Turn the heat up to medium-high on the grill.

2. Season salmon fillets with salt and pepper after brushing them with olive oil. Cook on the grill for 7–8 minutes on each side, or until done.

3. Prepare the quinoa in the veggie broth per the directions on the package.

4. Steam asparagus for a soft texture.

5. Present asparagus and quinoa beside grilled fish.

Nutritional values:

- Calories: 500 kcal
- Protein: 40 g
- Carbohydrates: 30 g
- Fat: 20 g

Chicken Curry with Brown Rice

- **Preparation time (P.T.):** 35 minutes
- **Ingredients (Ingr.):**
  - 300 g chicken breast, cubed
  - 200 g Greek yogurt
  - 30 g curry powder
  - 1 onion, diced (approximately 150 g)
  - 2 cloves garlic, minced (10 g)
  - 400 g diced tomatoes (canned)
  - 200 ml coconut milk
  - 180 g brown rice
  - 15 ml olive oil
  - Salt and pepper to taste
- **Servings (Serves):** 2
- **Mode of cooking:** Stovetop
- **Procedure:**

1. In a bowl, mix the chicken, Greek yogurt, and curry powder. For a minimum of half an hour, marinate.

2. Prepare brown rice as directed on the package.

3. In a pan over medium heat, preheat the olive oil. Add the garlic and onion, and cook until transparent.

4. Cook the marinated chicken until it turns golden brown on all sides.

5. Stir in the coconut milk and diced tomatoes. Once the chicken is cooked through, reduce heat to a simmer and cook

for 15 to 20 minutes.

6. Spoon brown rice over chicken curry.

Nutritional values:

- Calories: 500 kcal
- Protein: 35 g
- Carbohydrates: 50 g
- Fat: 20 g

Chicken Salad with Avocado and Walnuts

- **Preparation time (P.T.):** 15 minutes
- **Ingredients (Ingr.):**
    - 200 g cooked chicken breast, diced
    - 1 avocado, diced (approximately 150 g)
    - 50 g walnuts, chopped
    - 100 g cherry tomatoes, halved
    - 30 g red onion, thinly sliced
    - 30 ml olive oil
    - 15 ml lemon juice
    - Salt and pepper to taste
- **Servings (Serves):** 2
- **Mode of cooking:** No cooking required

- **Procedure:**

1. In a big bowl, mix together chicken, avocado, walnuts, cherry tomatoes, and red onion.

2. Combine lemon juice and olive oil in a small bowl. Add pepper and salt for seasoning.

3. Pour the salad with the dressing and toss to mix.

4. Serve right away.

Nutritional values:

- Calories: 400 kcal
- Protein: 30 g
- Carbohydrates: 15 g
- Fat: 25 g

Chocolate Banana Protein Smoothie

- **Preparation time (P.T.):** 5 minutes
- **Ingredients (Ingr.):**
    - 1 banana (approximately 120 g)
    - 30 g chocolate protein powder
    - 250 ml almond milk
    - 1 tsp cocoa powder (optional)

- o   1 tsp honey (optional)

- **Servings (Serves):** 1

- **Mode of cooking:** Blender

- **Procedure:**

1.   Combine all ingredients in a blender.

2.   Blend until smooth.

3.   Pour into a glass and serve immediately.

Nutritional values:

- o   Calories: 250 kcal

- o   Protein: 20 g

- o   Carbohydrates: 30 g

- o   Fat: 5 g

Baked Cod with Sweet Potatoes and Spinach

- **Preparation time (P.T.):** 30 minutes

- **Ingredients (Ingr.):**

  - o   2 cod fillets (approximately 200 g each)

  - o   400 g sweet potatoes, diced

  - o   200 g spinach, washed and chopped

  - o   30 ml olive oil

  - o   1 tsp garlic powder (5 g)

  - o   Salt and pepper to taste

- **Servings (Serves):** 2

- **Mode of cooking:** Oven and stovetop

- **Procedure:**

1.   Preheat oven to 375°F (190°C).

2.   Toss sweet potatoes with olive oil, garlic powder, salt, and pepper. Spread on a baking sheet and bake for 25 minutes or until tender.

3.   Meanwhile, season cod fillets with salt and pepper. Place on a baking sheet and bake for 10-12 minutes or until cooked.

4.   Steam spinach until wilted.

5.   Serve baked cod with sweet potatoes and spinach.

Nutritional values:

- o   Calories: 350 kcal

- o   Protein: 30 g

- o   Carbohydrates: 40 g

- o   Fat: 10 g

Turmeric Chicken with Steamed Vegetables

- **Preparation time (P.T.):** 30 minutes

- **Ingredients (Ingr.):**

    - 2 chicken breasts (approximately 300 g)

    - 1 tsp turmeric (5 g)

    - 1 tsp garlic powder (5 g)

    - 30 ml olive oil

    - 200 g broccoli florets

    - 200 g carrots, sliced

    - Salt and pepper to taste

- **Servings (Serves):** 2

- **Mode of cooking:** Stovetop and steaming

- **Procedure:**

1. Combine turmeric, garlic powder, salt, and pepper in a bowl. Rub the mixture over the chicken breasts.

2. Heat olive oil in a pan over medium heat. Cook chicken breasts for about 7-8 minutes per side or until cooked through.

3. Steam broccoli and carrots until tender.

4. Serve turmeric chicken with steamed vegetables.

Nutritional values:

- Calories: 350 kcal

- Protein: 35 g

- Carbohydrates: 15 g

- Fat: 15 g

Red Pepper and Onion Frittata

- **Preparation time (P.T.):** 20 minutes

- **Ingredients (Ingr.):**

    - 6 eggs (approximately 300 g)

    - 150 g red bell pepper, diced

    - 100 g onion, diced

    - 15 ml olive oil

    - Salt and pepper to taste

- **Servings (Serves):** 2

- **Mode of cooking:** Stovetop

- **Procedure:**

1. In a bowl, whisk the eggs with a pinch of salt and pepper.

2. Heat olive oil in a pan over medium heat. Add red bell pepper and onion, and cook until softened.

3. Pour eggs into the pan and cook until set. Fold the frittata in half and serve immediately.

Nutritional values:

- o Calories: 250 kcal

- o Protein: 20 g

- o Carbohydrates: 5 g

- o Fat: 18 g

Tuna Salad with Chickpeas and Peppers

- **Preparation time (P.T.):** 15 minutes

- **Ingredients (Ingr.):**

  - o 200 g canned tuna, drained

  - o 150 g chickpeas, rinsed and drained

  - o 150 g bell pepper, diced

  - o 100 g cherry tomatoes, halved

  - o 30 g red onion, thinly sliced

  - o 30 ml olive oil

  - o 15 ml lemon juice

  - o Salt and pepper to taste

- **Servings (Serves):** 2

- **Mode of cooking:** No cooking required

- **Procedure:**

1. Combine tuna, chickpeas, bell pepper, cherry tomatoes, and red onion in a large bowl.

2. In a small bowl, whisk together olive oil and lemon juice. Season with salt and pepper.

3. Drizzle the dressing over the salad and toss to combine.

4. Serve immediately.

Nutritional values:

- o Calories: 300 kcal

- o Protein: 25 g

- o Carbohydrates: 20 g

- o Fat: 15 g

Grilled Chicken with Avocado Sauce

- **Preparation time (P.T.):** 20 minutes

- **Ingredients (Ingr.):**

  - 2 chicken breasts (approximately 300 g)

  - 1 avocado, mashed (approximately 150 g)

  - 30 ml Greek yogurt

  - 15 ml lime juice

  - 1 clove garlic, minced (5 g)

  - 30 ml olive oil

  - Salt and pepper to taste

- **Servings (Serves):** 2

- **Mode of cooking:** Grill and no cooking required

- **Procedure:**

1. Preheat the grill to medium-high heat.

2. Brush chicken breasts with olive oil and season with salt and pepper. Grill for 7-8 minutes per side or until cooked through.

3. Combine mashed avocado, Greek yogurt, lime juice, garlic, salt, and pepper in a small bowl.

4. Serve grilled chicken with avocado sauce.

Nutritional values:

  - Calories: 350 kcal

  - Protein: 35 g

  - Carbohydrates: 10 g

  - Fat: 20 g

Egg White Frittata with Spinach and Green Onions

- **Preparation time (P.T.):** 15 minutes

- **Ingredients (Ingr.):**

  - 6 egg whites (approximately 200 g)

  - 100 g spinach, chopped

  - 50 g green onions, sliced

  - 15 ml olive oil

  - Salt and pepper to taste

- **Servings (Serves):** 2

- **Mode of cooking:** Stovetop

- **Procedure:**

1. In a bowl, whisk egg whites with a pinch of salt and pepper.

2. Heat olive oil in a pan over medium heat. Add spinach and green onions, cook until softened.

3. Pour egg whites into the pan and cook until set, stirring occasionally.

4. Serve immediately.

Nutritional values:

- o Calories: 150 kcal
- o Protein: 20 g
- o Carbohydrates: 5 g
- o Fat: 5 g

Shrimp Salad with Avocado and Grapefruit

- **Preparation time (P.T.):** 15 minutes
- **Ingredients (Ingr.):**
  - o 200 g cooked shrimp
  - o 1 avocado, diced (approximately 150 g)
  - o 1 grapefruit, segmented
  - o 100 g mixed greens
  - o 30 g red onion, thinly sliced
  - o 30 ml olive oil
  - o 15 ml lime juice
  - o Salt and pepper to taste
- **Servings (Serves):** 2
- **Mode of cooking:** No cooking required

- **Procedure:**

1. Combine shrimp, avocado, grapefruit segments, mixed greens, and red onion in a large bowl.

2. In a small bowl, whisk together olive oil and lime juice. Season with salt and pepper.

3. Drizzle the dressing over the salad and toss to combine.

4. Serve immediately.

Nutritional values:

- o Calories: 350 kcal
- o Protein: 25 g
- o Carbohydrates: 20 g
- o Fat: 20 g

Lemon Chicken Breast with Grilled Vegetables

- **Preparation time (P.T.):** 25 minutes
- **Ingredients (Ingr.):**
  - o 2 chicken breasts (approximately 300 g)
  - o 30 ml olive oil
  - o 1 lemon, juiced

- 1 bell pepper, sliced (approximately 150 g)
- 1 zucchini, sliced (approximately 200 g)
- 1 red onion, sliced (approximately 100 g)
- 1 tsp dried oregano (2 g)
- Salt and pepper to taste

- **Servings (Serves):** 2
- **Mode of cooking:** Grill and stovetop
- **Procedure:**

1. Preheat the grill to medium-high heat.

2. Mix olive oil, lemon juice, oregano, salt, and pepper in a small bowl.

3. Brush chicken breasts with the mixture and grill for 7-8 minutes per side or until cooked.

4. Toss sliced bell pepper, zucchini, and red onion with olive oil and grill until tender.

5. Serve the grilled chicken breast with grilled vegetables.

Nutritional values:

- Calories: 400 kcal
- Protein: 35 g
- Carbohydrates: 10 g
- Fat: 20 g

Chocolate Mint Protein Smoothie

- **Preparation time (P.T.):** 5 minutes
- **Ingredients (Ingr.):**
  - 1 banana (approximately 120 g)
  - 30 g chocolate protein powder
  - 250 ml almond milk
  - 10 mint leaves
  - 1 tsp cocoa powder (optional)
  - 1 tsp honey (optional)
- **Servings (Serves):** 1
- **Mode of cooking:** Blender
- **Procedure:**

1. Combine all ingredients in a blender.

2. Blend until smooth.

3. Pour into a glass and serve immediately.

Nutritional values:

- Calories: 250 kcal
- Protein: 20 g
- Carbohydrates: 30 g
- Fat: 5 g

Smoked Salmon with Arugula and Walnut Salad

- **Preparation time (P.T.):** 10 minutes

- **Ingredients (Ingr.):**

  - 150 g smoked salmon, sliced
  - 100 g arugula
  - 30 g walnuts, chopped
  - 1 avocado, sliced (approximately 150 g)
  - 100 g cherry tomatoes, halved
  - 30 ml olive oil
  - 15 ml lemon juice
  - Salt and pepper to taste

- **Servings (Serves):** 2

- **Mode of cooking:** No cooking required

- **Procedure:**

1. In a large bowl, combine arugula, walnuts, avocado, and cherry tomatoes.

2. Add smoked salmon slices on top.

3. In a small bowl, whisk together olive oil and lemon juice. Season with salt and pepper.

4. Drizzle the dressing over the salad and toss to combine.

5. Serve immediately.

Nutritional values:

- Calories: 350 kcal
- Protein: 20 g
- Carbohydrates: 10 g
- Fat: 25 g

Chicken Skewers with Yogurt and Cucumber Sauce

- **Preparation time (P.T.):** 30 minutes

- **Ingredients (Ingr.):**

  - 300 g chicken breast, cut into cubes
  - 15 ml olive oil
  - 1 tsp paprika (2 g)

- 1 tsp garlic powder (5 g)

- 200 g Greek yogurt

- 1 cucumber, grated (approximately 200 g)

- 1 clove garlic, minced (5 g)

- 15 ml lemon juice

- Salt and pepper to taste

- **Servings (Serves):** 2

- **Mode of cooking:** Grill

- **Procedure:**

1. Preheat the grill to medium-high heat.

2. In a bowl, Toss chicken cubes with olive oil, paprika, garlic powder, salt, and pepper.

3. Thread the chicken onto skewers and grill for 10-12 minutes, turning occasionally, until cooked.

4. In a small bowl, Mix Greek yogurt, grated cucumber, minced garlic, lemon juice, salt, and pepper.

5. Serve the chicken skewers with yogurt and cucumber sauce.

Nutritional values:

- Calories: 350 kcal

- Protein: 35 g

- Carbohydrates: 10 g

- Fat: 15 g

Tuna Salad with Green Beans and Boiled Eggs

- **Preparation time (P.T.):** 20 minutes

- **Ingredients (Ingr.):**

  - 200 g canned tuna, drained

  - 150 g green beans, trimmed and blanched

  - 2 boiled eggs, sliced (approximately 100 g)

  - 100 g cherry tomatoes, halved

  - 30 g red onion, thinly sliced

  - 30 ml olive oil

  - 15 ml lemon juice

  - Salt and pepper to taste

- **Servings (Serves):** 2

- **Mode of cooking:** No cooking required

- **Procedure:**

1. In a large bowl, combine tuna, green beans, boiled eggs, cherry tomatoes, and red onion.

2. In a small bowl, whisk together olive oil and lemon juice. Season with salt and pepper.

3. Drizzle the dressing over the salad and toss to combine.

4. Serve immediately.

Nutritional values:

- o Calories: 300 kcal
- o Protein: 25 g
- o Carbohydrates: 10 g
- o Fat: 20 g

Beef Steak with Cauliflower Puree

- **Preparation time (P.T.):** 30 minutes

- **Ingredients (Ingr.):**

  - o 2 beef steaks (approximately 200 g each)
  - o 30 ml olive oil
  - o 400 g cauliflower florets
  - o 50 ml heavy cream
  - o 1 clove garlic, minced (5 g)
  - o Salt and pepper to taste

- **Servings (Serves):** 2

- **Mode of cooking:** Grill and stovetop

- **Procedure:**

1. Preheat the grill to medium-high heat.

2. Brush steaks with olive oil and season with salt and pepper. Grill for about 5-7 minutes per side or until desired doneness.

3. Meanwhile, steam cauliflower until tender. Transfer to a blender, add heavy cream, garlic, salt, and pepper, and blend until smooth.

4. Serve grilled steak with cauliflower puree.

Nutritional values:

- o Calories: 450 kcal
- o Protein: 40 g
- o Carbohydrates: 10 g
- o Fat: 30 g

Vegetable Frittata with Low-Fat Cheese

- **Preparation time (P.T.):** 20 minutes

- **Ingredients (Ingr.):**

  - o 6 eggs (approximately 300 g)

- 150 g bell pepper, diced
- 100 g spinach, chopped
- 50 g low-fat cheese, shredded
- 15 ml olive oil
- Salt and pepper to taste

- **Servings (Serves):** 2

- **Mode of cooking:** Stovetop

- **Procedure:**

1. In a bowl, whisk the eggs with a pinch of salt and pepper.

2. Heat olive oil in a pan over medium heat. Add bell pepper and spinach and cook until softened.

3. Pour eggs into the pan and cook until set. Sprinkle cheese on top and fold the frittata in half.

4. Serve immediately.

Nutritional values:

- Calories: 300 kcal
- Protein: 25 g
- Carbohydrates: 10 g
- Fat: 20 g

Lentil Soup with Carrots and Celery

- **Preparation time (P.T.):** 40 minutes

- **Ingredients (Ingr.):**

  - 200 g lentils
  - 150 g carrots, sliced
  - 150 g celery, sliced
  - 100 g onion, diced
  - 2 cloves garlic, minced (10 g)
  - 1 liter vegetable broth
  - 30 ml olive oil
  - Salt and pepper to taste

- **Servings (Serves):** 4

- **Mode of cooking:** Stovetop

- **Procedure:**

1. Heat olive oil in a large pot over medium heat. Add onion and garlic, and sauté until softened.

2. Add carrots, celery, and lentils. Cook for 5 minutes.

3. Add vegetable broth and bring to a boil. Reduce heat and simmer for 30 minutes or until lentils are tender.

4. Season with salt and pepper to taste.

5.   Serve hot.

Nutritional values:

- o Calories: 250 kcal

- o Protein: 15 g

- o Carbohydrates: 35 g

- o Fat: 5 g

Green Smoothie with Spinach, Cucumber, and Apple

- **Preparation time (P.T.):** 5 minutes

- **Ingredients (Ingr.):**

  - o 100 g spinach

  - o 1 cucumber, chopped (approximately 200 g)

  - o 1 apple, cored and chopped (approximately 150 g)

  - o 250 ml almond milk

  - o 1 tsp honey (optional)

- **Servings (Serves):** 1

- **Mode of cooking:** Blender

- **Procedure:**

1.   Combine all ingredients in a blender.

2.   Blend until smooth.

3.   Pour into a glass and serve immediately.

Nutritional values:

- o Calories: 150 kcal

- o Protein: 5 g

- o Carbohydrates: 30 g

- o Fat: 3 g

Grilled Chicken with Mango Lime Sauce

- **Preparation time (P.T.):** 25 minutes

- **Ingredients (Ingr.):**

  - o 2 chicken breasts (approximately 300 g)

  - o 1 mango, peeled and diced (approximately 200 g)

  - o 30 ml lime juice

  - o 1 tsp honey (optional)

  - o 30 ml olive oil

  - o Salt and pepper to taste

- **Servings (Serves):** 2

- **Mode of cooking:** Grill and no cooking required

- **Procedure:**

1. Preheat the grill to medium-high heat.

2. Brush chicken breasts with olive oil and season with salt and pepper. Grill for 7-8 minutes per side or until cooked through.

3. In a blender, combine mango, lime juice, and honey (if using). Blend until smooth.

4. Serve grilled chicken with mango lime sauce.

Nutritional values:

- Calories: 300 kcal
- Protein: 35 g
- Carbohydrates: 20 g
- Fat: 10 g

Quinoa Salad with Shrimp and Avocado

- **Preparation time (P.T.):** 20 minutes

- **Ingredients (Ingr.):**

  - 200 g cooked shrimp
  - 180 g quinoa
  - 1 avocado, diced (approximately 150 g)
  - 100 g cherry tomatoes, halved
  - 30 g red onion, thinly sliced
  - 30 ml olive oil
  - 15 ml lime juice
  - Salt and pepper to taste

- **Servings (Serves):** 2

- **Mode of cooking:** Stovetop and no cooking required

- **Procedure:**

1. Cook quinoa according to package instructions.

2. Combine cooked shrimp, quinoa, avocado, cherry tomatoes, and red onion in a large bowl.

3. In a small bowl, whisk together olive oil and lime juice. Season with salt and pepper.

4. Drizzle the dressing over the salad and toss to combine.

5. Serve immediately.

Nutritional values:

- Calories: 400 kcal
- Protein: 25 g
- Carbohydrates: 40 g
- Fat: 15 g

Egg White Frittata with Spinach and Mushrooms

- **Preparation time (P.T.):** 15 minutes

- **Ingredients (Ingr.):**

    o 6 egg whites (approximately 200 g)

    o 150 g spinach, chopped

    o 150 g mushrooms, sliced

    o 15 ml olive oil

    o Salt and pepper to taste

- **Servings (Serves):** 2

- **Mode of cooking:** Stovetop

- **Procedure:**

1. Whisk egg whites with a pinch of salt and pepper in a bowl.

2. Heat olive oil in a pan over medium heat. Add spinach and mushrooms and cook until softened.

3. Pour egg whites into the pan and cook until set, stirring occasionally.

4. Serve immediately.

Nutritional values:

    o Calories: 150 kcal

    o Protein: 20 g

    o Carbohydrates: 5 g

    o Fat: 5 g

Walnut-crusted cod with Asparagus

- **Preparation time (P.T.):** 25 minutes

- **Ingredients (Ingr.):**

    o two cod fillets (approximately 200 g each)

    o 50 g walnuts, finely chopped

    o one egg, beaten (50 g)

    o 30 ml olive oil

    o 450 g asparagus, trimmed

    o Salt and pepper to taste

- **Servings (Serves):** 2

- **Mode of cooking:** Oven and stovetop

- **Procedure:**

1. Preheat oven to 375°F (190°C).

2. Dip cod fillets in the beaten egg, then coat with chopped walnuts.

3. Heat olive oil in a pan over medium heat. Brown cod fillets on both sides.

4. Transfer cod to a baking sheet and bake for 10 minutes or until cooked.

5. Steam asparagus until tender.

6. Serve walnut-crusted cod with steamed asparagus.

Nutritional values:

- Calories: 350 kcal
- Protein: 30 g
- Carbohydrates: 10 g
- Fat: 20 g

Chicken Curry with Cauliflower Rice

- **Preparation time (P.T.):** 30 minutes
- **Ingredients (Ingr.):**
  - 300 g chicken breast, cubed
  - 200 g Greek yogurt
  - 30 g curry powder
  - 1 onion, diced (approximately 150 g)
  - 2 cloves garlic, minced (10 g)
  - 400 g diced tomatoes (canned)
  - 200 ml coconut milk
  - 300 g cauliflower, riced
  - 15 ml olive oil
  - Salt and pepper to taste
- **Servings (Serves):** 2
- **Mode of cooking:** Stovetop
- **Procedure:**

1. Combine chicken, Greek yogurt, and curry powder in a bowl. Marinate for at least 30 minutes.

2. Heat olive oil in a pan over medium heat. Add onion and garlic, and sauté until translucent.

3. Add marinated chicken and cook until browned on all sides.

4. Stir in diced tomatoes and coconut milk. Bring to a simmer and cook for 15-20 minutes or until chicken is cooked through.

5. Meanwhile, steam cauliflower rice until tender.

6. Serve chicken curry over cauliflower rice.

Nutritional values:

- Calories: 400 kcal
- Protein: 35 g
- Carbohydrates: 20 g
- Fat: 20 g

Tuna Salad with Avocado and Cherry Tomatoes

- **Preparation time (P.T.):** 15 minutes

- **Ingredients (Ingr.):**

  - 200 g canned tuna, drained

  - 1 avocado, diced (approximately 150 g)

  - 100 g cherry tomatoes, halved

  - 30 g red onion, thinly sliced

  - 30 ml olive oil

  - 15 ml lemon juice

  - Salt and pepper to taste

- **Servings (Serves):** 2

- **Mode of cooking:** No cooking required

- **Procedure:**

1. Combine tuna, avocado, cherry tomatoes, and red onion in a large bowl.

2. In a small bowl, whisk together olive oil and lemon juice. Season with salt and pepper.

3. Drizzle the dressing over the salad and toss to combine.

4. Serve immediately.

Nutritional values:

  - Calories: 300 kcal

  - Protein: 25 g

  - Carbohydrates: 15 g

  - Fat: 20 g

Vanilla Peanut Butter Protein Smoothie

- **Preparation time (P.T.):** 5 minutes

- **Ingredients (Ingr.):**

  - 1 banana (approximately 120 g)

  - 30 g vanilla protein powder

  - 250 ml almond milk

  - 1 tbsp peanut butter (15 g)

- **Servings (Serves):** 1

- **Mode of cooking:** Blender

- **Procedure:**

1. Combine all ingredients in a blender.

2. Blend until smooth.

3. Pour into a glass and serve immediately.

Nutritional values:

- Calories: 300 kcal
- Protein: 20 g
- Carbohydrates: 30 g
- Fat: 10 g

Beef Steak with Mushroom Sauce

- **Preparation time (P.T.):** 30 minutes

- **Ingredients (Ingr.):**

  - 2 beef steaks (approximately 200 g each)
  - 200 g mushrooms, sliced
  - 1 onion, diced (approximately 150 g)
  - 2 cloves garlic, minced (10 g)
  - 30 ml olive oil
  - 50 ml beef broth
  - 30 ml heavy cream
  - Salt and pepper to taste

- **Servings (Serves):** 2

- **Mode of cooking:** Grill and stovetop

- **Procedure:**

1. Preheat the grill to medium-high heat.

2. Brush steaks with olive oil and season with salt and pepper. Grill 5-7 minutes per side or until desired doneness.

3. In a pan, heat olive oil over medium heat. Add onion and garlic, and sauté until softened.

4. Add mushrooms and cook until browned.

5. Stir in beef broth and heavy cream. Simmer until the sauce thickens.

6. Serve grilled steak with mushroom sauce.

Nutritional values:

- Calories: 500 kcal
- Protein: 35 g
- Carbohydrates: 10 g
- Fat: 35 g

Grilled Chicken with Tomato and Basil Salad

- **Preparation time (P.T.):** 20 minutes

- **Ingredients (Ingr.):**
  - 2 chicken breasts (approximately 300 g)
  - 200 g cherry tomatoes, halved
  - 30 g fresh basil leaves, chopped
  - 30 ml olive oil
  - 15 ml balsamic vinegar
  - Salt and pepper to taste
- **Servings (Serves):** 2
- **Mode of cooking:** Grill and no cooking required
- **Procedure:**

1. Preheat grill to medium-high heat.

2. Brush chicken breasts with olive oil and season with salt and pepper. Grill for about 7-8 minutes per side, or until cooked through.

3. In a bowl, combine cherry tomatoes and basil.

4. In a small bowl, whisk together olive oil and balsamic vinegar. Season with salt and pepper.

5. Drizzle the dressing over the tomato and basil salad, toss to combine.

6. Serve grilled chicken with tomato and basil salad.

Nutritional values:
  - Calories: 300 kcal
  - Protein: 35 g
  - Carbohydrates: 10 g
  - Fat: 15 g

Spinach and Onion Frittata

- **Preparation time (P.T.):** 20 minutes
- **Ingredients (Ingr.):**
  - 6 eggs (approximately 300 g)
  - 150 g spinach, chopped
  - 100 g onion, diced
  - 15 ml olive oil
  - Salt and pepper to taste
- **Servings (Serves):** 2
- **Mode of cooking:** Stovetop
- **Procedure:**

1. Beat the eggs in a bowl with a dash of pepper and salt.

2. In a pan over medium heat, preheat the olive oil. Cook the onion and spinach until they are tender.

3. Add the eggs to the pan and cook them until they set. Serve the frittata right away after folding it in half.

Nutritional values:

- o   Calories: 250 kcal
- o   Protein: 20 g
- o   Carbohydrates: 5 g
- o   Fat: 18 g

Grilled Salmon with Avocado Sauce

- **Preparation time (P.T.):** 25 minutes
- **Ingredients (Ingr.):**
  - o   2 salmon fillets (approximately 200 g each)
  - o   1 avocado, mashed (approximately 150 g)
  - o   30 ml Greek yogurt
  - o   15 ml lime juice
  - o   1 clove garlic, minced (5 g)
  - o   30 ml olive oil
  - o   Salt and pepper to taste
- **Servings (Serves):** 2
- **Mode of cooking:** Grill and no cooking required

- **Procedure:**

1. Turn the grill's heat up to medium-high.

2. Season salmon fillets with salt and pepper after brushing them with olive oil. Cook on the grill for 7–8 minutes on each side, or until well done.

3. Combine Greek yogurt, mashed avocado, lime juice, garlic, salt, and pepper in a small bowl.

4. Top grilled salmon with a sauce made of avocados.

Nutritional values:

- o   Calories: 400 kcal
- o   Protein: 35 g
- o   Carbohydrates: 10 g
- o   Fat: 25 g

Chicken Salad with Mango and Lime

- **Preparation time (P.T.):** 15 minutes
- **Ingredients (Ingr.):**
  - o   200 g cooked chicken breast, diced
  - o   1 mango, diced (approximately 200 g)

- o 100 g cherry tomatoes, halved
- o 30 g red onion, thinly sliced
- o 30 ml olive oil
- o 15 ml lime juice
- o Salt and pepper to taste
- **Servings (Serves):** 2
- **Mode of cooking:** No cooking required
- **Procedure:**

1. Combine chicken, mango, cherry tomatoes, and red onion in a big bowl.

2. Combine lime juice and olive oil in a small bowl. Add pepper and salt for seasoning.

3. Pour the salad with the dressing and toss to mix.Serve immediately.

Nutritional values:

- o Calories: 300 kcal
- o Protein: 25 g
- o Carbohydrates: 20 g
- o Fat: 15 g

Chocolate Mint Protein Smoothie

- **Preparation time (P.T.):** 5 minutes

- **Ingredients (Ingr.):**
  - o 1 banana (approximately 120 g)
  - o 30 g chocolate protein powder
  - o 250 ml almond milk
  - o 10 mint leaves
  - o 1 tsp cocoa powder (optional)
  - o 1 tsp honey (optional)
- **Servings (Serves):** 1
- **Mode of cooking:** Blender
- **Procedure:**

1. Combine all ingredients in a blender.

2. Blend until smooth.

3. Pour into a glass and serve immediately.

Nutritional values:

- o Calories: 250 kcal
- o Protein: 20 g
- o Carbohydrates: 30 g
- o Fat: 5 g

Grilled Chicken with Honey Mustard Sauce

- **Preparation time (P.T.):** 20 minutes

- **Ingredients (Ingr.):**

  - 2 chicken breasts (approximately 300 g)

  - 30 ml honey

  - 30 ml Dijon mustard

  - 15 ml olive oil

  - Salt and pepper to taste

- **Servings (Serves):** 2

- **Mode of cooking:** Grill and no cooking required

- **Procedure:**

1. Turn the grill's heat up to medium-high.

2. Season chicken breasts with salt and pepper after brushing them with olive oil. Cook on the grill for 7–8 minutes on each side, or until well done.

3. Combine honey and Dijon mustard in a small bowl.

4. Present the chicken grilled with a honey mustard sauce.

Nutritional values:

  - Calories: 300 kcal

  - Protein: 35 g

  - Carbohydrates: 15 g

  - Fat: 10 g

Zucchini and Green Onion Frittata

- **Preparation time (P.T.):** 20 minutes

- **Ingredients (Ingr.):**

  - 6 eggs (approximately 300 g)

  - 150 g zucchini, diced

  - 100 g green onions, sliced

  - 15 ml olive oil

  - Salt and pepper to taste

- **Servings (Serves):** 2

- **Mode of cooking:** Stovetop

- **Procedure:**

1. Beat the eggs in a bowl with a dash of pepper and salt.

2. In a pan over medium heat, preheat the olive oil. When the zucchini and green onions are soft, add them and simmer.

3. Add the eggs to the pan and cook them until they set. Serve the frittata right away after folding it in half.

Nutritional values:

- o Calories: 250 kcal
- o Protein: 20 g
- o Carbohydrates: 5 g
- o Fat: 18 g

Tuna Salad with Chickpeas and Peppers

- **Preparation time (P.T.):** 15 minutes

- **Ingredients (Ingr.):**

  - o 200 g canned tuna, drained
  - o 150 g chickpeas, rinsed and drained
  - o 150 g bell pepper, diced
  - o 100 g cherry tomatoes, halved
  - o 30 g red onion, thinly sliced
  - o 30 ml olive oil
  - o 15 ml lemon juice
  - o Salt and pepper to taste

- **Servings (Serves):** 2

- **Mode of cooking:** No cooking required

- **Procedure:**

1. Put the bell pepper, cherry tomatoes, red onion, chickpeas, and tuna in a big bowl.

2. Combine lemon juice and olive oil in a small bowl. Add pepper and salt for seasoning.

3. Pour the salad with the dressing and toss to mix..

4. Serve immediately.

Nutritional values:

- o Calories: 300 kcal
- o Protein: 25 g
- o Carbohydrates: 20 g
- o Fat: 15 g

Beef Steak with Herb Sauce

- **Preparation time (P.T.):** 25 minutes

- **Ingredients (Ingr.):**

  - o 2 beef steaks (approximately 200 g each)
  - o 30 ml olive oil

- 1 tsp dried thyme (2 g)
  - 1 tsp dried rosemary (2 g)
  - 1 clove garlic, minced (5 g)
  - 50 ml beef broth
  - 30 ml heavy cream
  - Salt and pepper to taste

- **Servings (Serves):** 2

- **Mode of cooking:** Grill and stovetop

- **Procedure:**

1. Turn the grill's heat up to medium-high.

2. Season steaks with salt and pepper after brushing them with olive oil. Grill to desired doneness, about 5 to 7 minutes per side.

3. Heat the olive oil in a pan over medium heat. Saute the garlic, thyme, and rosemary until aromatic.Add beef broth and heavy cream, simmer until sauce thickens.

4. Serve grilled steak with herb sauce.

Nutritional values:

  - Calories: 450 kcal
  - Protein: 35 g
  - Carbohydrates: 5 g
  - Fat: 30 g

EXTRA CONTENTS

90-Day Meal Plan

Daily Plan for Muscle Building

Detailed tables with nutritional values.

Personal stories explaining the inspiration behind specific recipes

Energizing Protein and Diet Breads